I0821230

— 150 —
LIBRARIES
YOU NEED TO VISIT BEFORE — YOU DIE —

By Léa Teuscher

Back cover image George Peabody Library:
Jason Varney

Lannoo

I have always imagined Paradise will be a kind of library.

— Jorge Luis Borges

Will you be reading this book in a library? I hope some of you will, or that it will inspire you to think about this marvellous concept, which encompasses both precious collections and the building they are housed in. From the International Space Station to Antarctica, they are pretty much everywhere – including in an old cupboard in someone's front garden on a street near you. Whether you love them for containing all human knowledge, beautifully organised and classified, or because they offer the excitement of discovering a new favourite book – somewhere there is a library for you.

As sure as books pile up on the bedside tables of avid readers, new public libraries open to answer the ever-evolving needs of their times. In the following pages we visit opulent baroque monasteries in central Europe and conceptual spaces in Asia; we stop at contemporary hubs in the heart of communities from Peru to Sydney; and we look at innovative spaces made on a shoestring that spread the joy of reading among younger readers from South America to Africa.

Whether they are cathedrals of knowledge designed by leading architects, or simpler neighbourhood branches, libraries are the third spaces where individuals meet society, and cultural exchange blossoms. At the library, people from very different backgrounds meet up to attend events, use a 3D printer or learn essential skills. Despite – or because of – the digitalisation of our world, libraries are far from dusty relics, but interactive, innovative places that offer a world of possibilities.

As symbols of the power of learning, they can be the key to democracy, or become battlegrounds for culture wars, their books banned and sometimes burnt. Or, they might be safe and cosy spaces where public debate thrives and creative gatherings abound. Interestingly, the idea of borrowing and sharing, rather than buying, also offers a greener, less wasteful way of enjoying books (and, increasingly, other items such as tools, toys and musical instruments).

In honour of the great librarians who make these spaces come alive with their recommendations and exhibitions, here are my suggestions for further reading. For fiction, delve into Umberto Eco's *The Name of the Rose* and its maze-like Secretum library; for art, a monograph by photographer Andreas Gursky; for architecture, Campbell and Pryce's *The Library*; and for history, der Weduwen and Pettegree's *The Library: A Fragile History*. Last but not least is the children's section, with Roald Dahl's *Matilda*, a gleeful celebration of the library as a place of refuge, and of the power of books.

OVERVIEW

EUROPE

OVERVIEW

OVERVIEW

THE AMERICAS

OVERVIEW

OCEANIA

AFRICA AND THE MIDDLE EAST

01 UTOPIA

Utopia 1, 9300 Aalst, Belgium

TO VISIT
BEFORE YOU DIE
BECAUSE

A highly sustainable building on a tricky urban site, this spacious minimalist library celebrates the beauty of local bricks.

Named after Thomas More's 1516 classic, *Utopia*, first printed by prominent Aalst citizen Dirk Martens, this sustainably built library was designed by KAAN Architecten and opened in 2018. It's worth a visit to admire how the new building has been slotted into the urban fabric of the city centre, with the 8,000 sq m brick structure incorporating a 19th-century school and interacting with the surrounding buildings. Three new public squares surround the beautifully detailed library, where brickwork dialogues with light-grey concrete elements. There is a café, an auditorium and an atrium reading room with cantilevered floors and 11.5m-high bookcases that stretch towards the ceiling, some filled with books donated by the residents of Aalst. Although there are ballet and music lessons just above in the Academy for Performing Arts, it's a peaceful space that has become the city's living room. The 10,000 new patrons who have joined since its opening (10 times the normal rate) might even say that it is the ideal library.

aalst.bibliotheek.be

+32 53 723 851

02 DOKK1

Hack Kampmanns Plads 2, 8000 Aarhus Centrum, Denmark

TO VISIT BEFORE YOU DIE BECAUSE

One of Denmark's most visited cultural destinations, Dokk1 restores the city's connection to the waterfront, and opens up a world of possibilities for its citizens.

Admired around the world for their style and functionality, Danish public buildings are designed to make people's lives better, and that's exactly what Aarhus' Dokk1 library and citizen service hub aims to do. Located on the city's waterfront, the futuristic glass prism was designed by architects Schmidt Hammer Lassen and Kristine Jensen to be transparent, making all activities within visible from the outside and providing views across the harbour and city. Surrounded by irregular staircases and colourful playgrounds designed by specialists Monstrum to bring the lessons of the library to life, it is home to a series of wooden atriums and interconnected meeting spaces that promote democracy and a sense of community. It is alive with activity all day long; people come here to renew their passport, attend one of the 1,500 events and activities organised every year or simply read by a window overlooking the bay. Shaped by the people who use it every day, Dokk1 is constantly evolving, and recently opened a media lab designed to help young people navigate the digital world.

dokk1.dk/english

+45 89 409 200

03 ADMONT MONASTERY LIBRARY

Kirchplatz 1, 8911 Admont, Austria

TO VISIT BEFORE YOU DIE BECAUSE

Featuring secret staircases and jaw-dropping frescoes, this 73m-long white-and-gold library is one of the great masterpieces of European Late Baroque.

Constructed between 1764 and 1774, the Admont Monastery Library was designed by the Austrian architect Josef Hueber, a proponent of the Enlightenment who said that 'light should fill the room as well as the mind'. It's an enormous space with a dizzying geometric pattern on the floor, and it is very bright indeed – even the books are white. Apparently, the abbot ordered them to be rebound in white pigskin, at enormous expense, to match the shelves. The top ones are reached using special stepladders or cleverly concealed staircases. The monastery's collection comprises around 200,000 volumes (60,000 of which are in the main hall), including 1,400 manuscripts and 530 incunabula. The library's seven ceiling domes were painted from 1775 to 1776 by Bartolomeo Altomonte, who was 80 years old at the time. A central dome focuses on divine wisdom, while the others are dedicated to themes such as history, theology, medicine and the fine arts. Predating the library but placed at its centre are wooden statues painted to look like bronze and representing the Four Last Things: Death, Judgement, Heaven and Hell.

stiftadmont.at +43 36 132 312 604

04 HENDRIK CONSCIENCE LIBRARY

Hendrik Conscienceplein 4, 2000 Antwerp, Belgium

TO VISIT BEFORE YOU DIE BECAUSE

On a charming square in Antwerp, this historic Flemish collection is showcased in a 1930s library housed in a 17th-century Jesuit building.

Printing presses were introduced to the Low Countries in the mid-1470s, leading to a boom in book trade that would soon turn Antwerp into a major centre for printers and booksellers. Just a few years later, in 1481, the Hendrik Conscience Library was born, following a donation of 41 books. Today it holds more than 1.5 million volumes and is considered one of the best Flemish heritage collections (it is named after Hendrik Conscience, author of the very first Flemish novel, *In the Year of Miracles*). The first 150,000 items in the catalogue are preserved in the Nottebohm Room, a charming library with dark wooden bookcases and metal galleries dating from 1936. Open to visitors during the summer, or for exhibitions, events and guided tours, it contains the oldest item in the collection (an Egyptian papyrus protected from view) as well as two Blaeu globes and a statue of Plantin. You can learn more about the printer and see his library in the wonderful Plantin-Moretus Museum on the other side of town.

conscience bibliotheek.be +32 33 388 710

05 GABRIEL GARCÍA MÁRQUEZ LIBRARY

Plaça de Carmen Balcells Segalà, 1, Districte Sant Martí, 08020 Barcelona, Spain

TO VISIT BEFORE YOU DIE BECAUSE

Recognised as the best public library in the world in 2023, this pioneering neighbourhood library is now known as the 'Guggenheim of La Verneda'.

From a car park behind a police station to one of the world's best libraries – Biblioteca Gabriel García Márquez, the third largest of Barcelona's 40 libraries, appeared from nowhere in 2022 to become the beating heart of the Sant Martí district. Specialising in Latin American literature, it is named after the Colombian writer Gabriel García Márquez, who lived in the Catalan capital in the 1970s and wrote *The Autumn of the Patriarch* here. It was designed by Suma Arquitectura following a long collaboration with the local library services, with the aim 'to reclaim libraries as paradigms of public space, authentic catalysts and social condensers'. Mission accomplished with a much-loved, six-storey building that cantilevers over an outdoor urban lounge framed by magnificent trees. Evoking stacked books with folded pages, the library comes with a triangular courtyard and oblique angles inspired by Eixample's diagonal streets, its sharpness softened by the warmth of the exposed, LEED Gold timber structure. It is home to the collection of cartoonist Francisco Ibáñez, as well as cosy lounges with hanging seats, hidden nooks and wooden platforms.

ajuntament.barcelona.cat/biblioteques/ca/bibgarciamarquez

+34 930 026 512

06 JACOB AND WILHELM GRIMM CENTRE

Geschwister-Scholl-Straße 1/3, 10117 Berlin, Germany

TO VISIT
BEFORE YOU DIE
BECAUSE

Located on Berlin's cultural mile, Humboldt University's imposing main library takes its design cues from the repetitive rhythm created by rows of bookshelves.

Opened in 2009, the year Humboldt University celebrated its 200th anniversary, the Jacob and Wilhelm Grimm Centre is named after the Grimm Brothers, the academics and folklore experts known for their dark fairy tales. Their private library, consisting of around 6,000 volumes – many annotated with personal notes and entries – can be found on the building's sixth floor. The rest of the centre's 2-million-item-strong collection focuses on the topics of humanities, social sciences, cultural studies and economics. But it's the bookcases rather than the books that form the inspiration for Swiss architect Max Dudler's award-winning design, with a basic 1.5m grid reflecting the centre spacing of the black shelving. Clad inside and out in pale-yellow Jura limestone, the geometric building is home to a cathedral-like reading room and serene workspaces where every reader gets a window seat with views of the Berlin skyline. Splashes of red, green linoleum desktops, cherry wood veneer and walnut parquet add colour and texture to the minimalist spaces.

ub.hu-berlin.de/en/locations +49 30 209 399 370

07 PHILOLOGICAL LIBRARY

Freie Universität Berlin, Habelschwerdter Allee 45, 14195 Berlin, Germany

TO VISIT BEFORE YOU DIE BECAUSE

Shaped like a brain, this energy-efficient university library by Foster + Partners is protected by an innovative curved aluminium and steel bubble.

The largest of Berlin's three universities, Freie Universität Berlin is located on a 1970s campus by innovative architects Candilis, Josic, Woods and Schiedhelm and nicknamed the rust bucket thanks to a Corten-steel façade designed by Jean Prouvé. The modernist buildings were renovated by Foster + Partners, who also combined six separate courtyards to create the new Philological Library in 2005. Replacing 11 libraries and focusing on topics such as linguistics, comparative literature and philosophy, the new central library features four undulating mezzanines shaped like the two hemispheres of the human brain. The entire thing is wrapped in a high-tech, double-skin bubble. 'An inner membrane of translucent glass fibre filters sunlight and creates an atmosphere of concentration, while scattered window openings create changing patterns of light and shade, with momentary view of the sky and glimpses of sunlight,' writes architect Norman Foster. The building is also home to a 'library within a library', an installation by Li Silberberg, spanning over twenty years of the artist's diaries and sketchbooks, presented in a large glass box.

fu-berlin.de/en/sites/philbib +49 30 83 858 888

08 BERLIN STATE LIBRARY

Unter den Linden 8, 10117 Berlin/Potsdamer Platz 33, 10785 Berlin, Germany

TO VISIT BEFORE YOU DIE BECAUSE

This is 'one library with two homes', a city institution now reunited and spanning two equally imposing buildings with completely different aesthetics.

Known by locals as the Stabi, the Berlin State Library offers a double dose of stunning architecture: the Unter den Linden branch to the west, and the Potsdamer Platz library to the east. The first, a grand neo-baroque 1913 building, was badly damaged during the war and has been beautifully restored. The magnificent original staircase now leads to its Atlantis reading room, a vast atrium lined with red carpet, built in the ruins of the old dome. This branch focuses on materials published before 1945 and is home to a museum with treasures such as a giant globe from 1826 and the original score for J.S. Bach's Mass in B minor. On nearby Bebelplatz is Micha Ullman's collection of empty subterranean bookcases remembering the Nazi book burnings that took place here in 1933. The Berlin State Library's other branch is in Hans Scharoun's 1970s behemoth, an iconic building with a golden façade, circular skylights and walls of coloured glass blocks. It is here that angels walk among the readers, listening to their thoughts, in Wim Wenders' classic film *Wings of Desire*.

staatsbibliothek-berlin.de/en +49 30 266 433888

09 LIBRARY OF BIRMINGHAM

Centenary Square, Broad Street, Birmingham B1 2ND, UK

TO VISIT BEFORE YOU DIE BECAUSE

Uniting the 'written and the spoken word', this library and theatre is an ode to the circle, wrapped in a delicate filigree façade inspired by the city's crafts and industries.

This blue-and-gold library was built in 2013 at the heart of the UK's second city, a fascinating melting pot of culture and architecture. Beautiful to look at from both the outside and inside, its intricate façade comprises over 5,000 interlocking metal circles. This geometric shape informs Mecanoo's design of the entire building and references the city's jewellery heritage, steel industry and perhaps even *The Lord of the Rings* (author J.R.R. Tolkien grew up nearby). Statement escalators link eight rotundas, including a golden case for the library's Victorian Shakespeare Memorial Room perched on the roof. Linked to the refurbished 1960s REP Theatre, the new building cantilevers to create a canopy and garden 'balcony' with views of the square below. Instead of being hidden in the basement (home to the music and children's library, with a large outdoor amphitheatre), the archives are proudly on display. Collection highlights include drawings by inventor James Watt, as well as a special music collection featuring local bands such as Black Sabbath, UB40, Duran Duran and The Streets.

birmingham.gov.uk/libraryofbirmingham +44 121 242 4242

10 METROPOLITAN ERVIN SZABÓ LIBRARY

Szabó Ervin tér 1, Budapest 1088, Hungary

TO VISIT BEFORE YOU DIE BECAUSE

Named after its first director, social scientist Ervin Szabó, this 'palace of books' features luxurious reading rooms in a 19th-century mansion.

Jutting forwards like the prow of a large ship at the junction of Budapest's Baross and Reviczky Streets is the prestigious Wenckheim Palace, a neo-baroque mansion once home to 11 halls, 48 rooms and 5 kitchens. Designed in the 1880s by Artúr Meinig, it has been home to the Hungarian capital's public library since 1931, when bespoke shelving and cabinets in the style of the original palace were added to the grand halls, and private apartments were converted into fireproof book storage areas. Despite sustaining heavy damage during the war, the original splendour of the building was perfectly restored in the 2000s, the great halls liberated from their furniture and the library extended into an adjoining historic house and a new eight-storey building. Head to the fourth floor to marvel at the carved figures, Rococo decorations and Venetian crystal chandeliers; the Wenckheim family dining room is now the art book reading room. There's also a café in the former carriage house off the beautiful, yellow covered courtyard.

fszek.hu +36 14 115 000

11 WREN LIBRARY

Trinity Street, Cambridge CB2 1TQ, UK

TO VISIT
BEFORE YOU DIE
BECAUSE

Flooded with natural light and filled with literary treasures, Christopher Wren's masterpiece for Trinity College is the earliest example of an alcove library.

Cambridge has some of the finest 18th-century libraries in the world, but few are accessible to the public. Thankfully, the Wren Library, a working library at the heart of Trinity College, is open to visitors for a couple of hours every weekday. Designed by Christopher Wren in 1695, it forms one end of an elegant courtyard next to the River Cam and was built on the first floor to avoid flooding. Featuring a chequered marble floor, carvings by Grinling Gibbons and busts of famous writers, the rectangular room is taller than usual, with the bookshelves (also designed by Wren) positioned underneath 13 large windows and arranged to form alcoves – a revolutionary layout at the time. Considered a distraction to scholars in the 19th century, a 1775 stained-glass window by Giovanni Cipriani, depicting the muse of the college presenting Isaac Newton to King George III, was once hidden by thick curtains. Lift the protective covers of the exhibition cases to admire a changing display of some of the library's treasures, which include early editions of Shakespeare, works by alumni including Byron, Tennyson and A.A. Milne, and intriguing artefacts such as a lock of Newton's hair.

trin.cam.ac.uk/library

12 JOANINA LIBRARY

Paço das Escolas (Entrance on R. Dr. Guilherme Moreira), 3000-233 Coimbra, Portugal

TO VISIT BEFORE YOU DIE BECAUSE

The finest example of Portuguese Baroque, this former university library boasts rich decorations as well as hidden ladders and staircases.

Completed in 1728, the Biblioteca Joanina is named in honour of King John V, whose portrait, painted by Domenico Duprà, is placed at the heart of the building's piano nobile. The painted king watches over three halls ornamented with rich carvings and gold paintings. They are each a different colour (black, red and green) and connected by a series of wooden archways painted to look like marble. They hide stairs up to the intricate wooden galleries, which frame a trompe l'œil ceiling. Wooden ladders camouflaged in between the bookshelves can be pulled out to reach the top shelves, while cosy studies with beautiful views hide behind the bookcases on the lower level. The collection of 60,000 books, representing the best of what was printed throughout Europe between the 15th and 18th centuries, can still be consulted by researchers today. Designed primarily to preserve the precious books, the building has 2m-thick exterior walls; you can see its beautiful stone arches on the Middle Floor. And just like in Mafra (page 48), colonies of bats have lived here for centuries.

visit.uc.pt/en/space-list/joanina +351 239 242 744

13 THE BLACK DIAMOND

Søren Kierkegaards Plads 1, 1221 Copenhagen, Denmark

TO VISIT
BEFORE YOU DIE
BECAUSE

Sitting on the edge of Copenhagen Harbour, Denmark's national library combines classic and contemporary spaces, including a showstopping atrium.

The Royal Danish Library's central Copenhagen location comprises a historic 1906 library, home to a copy of Charlemagne's Palace Chapel in Aachen Cathedral, linked by three bridges to a 1999 building by architects Schmidt Hammer Lassen. Clad in dark marble and glass and known as the Black Diamond, it is formed of two tilted cubes that reflect the waters of the harbour. From its glazed atrium, a warm space with sinuous galleries and long escalators, you can catch glimpses of Christianshavn. The library holds nearly all known Danish printed works, including the first Danish books, printed in 1482 by Johann Snell. Its galleries house the country's first permanent display on the history of portrait photography, as well as a Treasures exhibition featuring Hans Christian Andersen's diary and Karen Blixen's manuscripts. Guided tours are held every Monday, while children's activities include a treasure hunt through the library in search of the Diamond of Wisdom. There's also a garden, bookshop, concert hall and a harbourside café serving coffee, rye bread toast and cinnamon buns.

kb.dk/en/visit-us

+45 33 474 747

14 TRINITY COLLEGE LIBRARY

Trinity College Dublin, The University of Dublin, College Green, Dublin 2, D02 PN40, Ireland

TO VISIT BEFORE YOU DIE BECAUSE

Located in the heart of Dublin, this magnificent library is known for its atmospheric Long Room and medieval illuminated manuscript, the Book of Kells.

A major tourist attraction, Trinity College Library uses digital projections and beautiful contemporary displays to highlight its historic treasures, including the lavishly illustrated Book of Kells. Visit an exhibition focusing on the monks who created the 9th-century gospel manuscript and the symbolism and artistry found in its 340 illuminated folios, then see the book itself. Two pages are rotated every 12 weeks, so you can marvel at the bold and expert script known as 'insular majuscule', written on vellum and accompanied by abstract decorations and images of plants and animals. Upstairs is the Long Room, home to 200,000 of the library's oldest books. Although the building was completed in 1732, the library that we see today, with its distinctive barrel vault ceiling, dates from 1856, when architects Deane and Woodward completely remodelled the space. It is now being restored as part of a huge conservation project, so to make up for its closure, there is a temporary digital exhibition pavilion where visitors can immerse themselves in the Secret Life of the Collections, the Book of Kells 360 and the Long Room Reimagined.

visittrinity.ie +353 18 962 308

15 OODI

Töölönlahdenkatu 4, 00100 Helsinki, Finland

TO VISIT BEFORE YOU DIE BECAUSE

'The flagship library for a nation of booklovers', this lively meeting place opened in 2018 and offers innovative services right at the heart of the Finnish capital.

At Helsinki's Oodi you can try virtual reality glasses, make music, digitise old photos, play chess or even paint northern lights on a fairy tale wall, all in a breathtaking building designed by ALA Architects. Named after the Finnish word for 'ode' (chosen from 1,600 suggestions from the public), it's a fun space to explore, with a cinema, workshops with 3D printers and vinyl cutters, a games room with the newest video gaming consoles and a reading room where you can settle down with a coffee and one of the 70,000 books on offer, under a ceiling resembling clouds. It is also a symbol for equality located opposite the Finnish Parliament House. 'Everyone is welcome at Oodi, and equality is the most important of the library's values – together with freedom of expression,' says its director Anna-Maria Soininvaara. 'Oodi offers something for everyone that is worth leaving the house for – an opportunity to be inspired by new experiences every day.' Oodi's mission is also to trial new services; the most successful are then replicated across the country. The nearby 1840s National Library of Finland is also worth a visit.

oodihelsinki.fi +358 931 085 000

Skogen berikar
ditt liv

16 RIKHARDINKATU LIBRARY

Rikhardinkatu 3, 00130 Helsinki, Finland

TO VISIT BEFORE YOU DIE BECAUSE

A source of inspiration and knowledge since its opening in 1882, this elegant yet homely library specialises in art books through its RikArt collection.

There's no shortage of amazing libraries in the Nordic countries. From Norway to Denmark, it seems every town is blessed with a stylish, wood-lined library. And it all started here at Rikhardinkatu Library in Helsinki, the first building in the region specifically designed to serve as a public library. Helsinki's main public library until 1986, the neo-Renaissance building is the work of leading Finnish architect Theodor Höijer, with some 1920s additions by architect Runar Eklund. Books are displayed all around a central atrium, its various floors linked by a beautiful spiral staircase. Specialities include an excellent children's section, as well as a strong focus on art. A changing exhibition displays some of the unique artists' books of the RikArt collection, established in 2000. Defying strict definitions, they challenge traditional assumptions about the shape and content of books, and include wonderful items such as a cut-out, concertina piece by Marianne Laimer (*Inside my head*, 2013) or a book with a pebble hidden inside by Priya Pereira (*Stone*, 2012). The library's courtyard is decorated with colourful umbrellas and welcomes readers, outdoor chess players and special events in the summer.

helmet.finna.fi @rikartbooks +358 931 085 013

17 LIBRARY IN THE WOODS

A841, Forest of the Falls, Isle of Arran, KA27 8RR, Scotland, UK

TO VISIT BEFORE YOU DIE BECAUSE

Set in a fairy tale forest on a Scottish island, this log cabin library is filled with tens of thousands of notes by readers from around the world.

After he lost 300 trees during the Boxing Day storms of 1998, Albert Holmes decided to mill the fallen trees and build a library with the help of his friends at Eas Mor Ecology, an organisation aiming to convert the Isle of Arran's conifer plantations into more natural woodland. They cut a path through the 16-hectare forest, constructed a log cabin with a green roof, and left some books, pencils and paper for rainy days. Built with love by volunteers, the small library was meant to teach people about ecology and the surrounding woods. It seemed to have struck a chord with visitors: there are now 25 layers of notes, poems and drawings pinned to its walls. 'If you ever come to see it, it will touch your soul,' says Albert about the library, which was recently refurbished. It has a special kind of energy, and you can spend hours reading the notes before continuing your hike to the nearby amphitheatre, waterfall and viewing platforms. Then stop for a simple lunch or a cup of tea at the lovely café, furnished with beautifully crafted wooden furniture and sculptures.

@easmorecology

18 OSCAR NIEMEYER LIBRARY

2 place Oscar Niemeyer, 76600 Le Havre, France

TO VISIT BEFORE YOU DIE BECAUSE

One of Oscar Niemeyer's two volcano-shaped buildings in Le Havre, a once dormant hall has been turned into a stylish cultural hub now bustling with readers.

Oscar Niemeyer originally conceived the Petit Volcan (Little Volcano) as a multipurpose cultural hall, a 'liveable sculpture' with curved slopes rising amidst the modernist apartment blocks of Auguste Perret, in a city completely rebuilt after the Second World War. In 2006, the leading Brazilian architect gave the green light for the transformation of the Maison de la Culture into a lively new library with a rich programme of events. Architects Françoise Sogno and Deshoulières Jeanneau let natural light flow into the concrete circular space with skylights and portholes, installing a winter garden for the periodical section along a curved wall, and adding a wooden staircase in the crater of the 'volcano'. The 5,000 sq m space houses 114,000 items, from novels to manga and children's books, which can be enjoyed in a huge variety of seating areas, including banquettes, pebble-shaped floor cushions and rugs. The salon Niemeyer is home to classic leather armchairs and design pieces, while the café offers local specialities. Niemeyer designed only two other libraries, Victor Civita in São Paulo and Duque de Caxias in Rio de Janeiro.

bibliotheques.lehavre.fr

+33 235 197 000

19 UNIVERSITY LIBRARY OF LEUVEN

KU Leuven Libraries, Mgr. Ladeuzeplein 21,
3000 Leuven, Belgium

TO VISIT BEFORE YOU DIE BECAUSE

Rebuilt in 1950, this university library is a wooden box of delights with beautifully carved details inspired by the passions of its Belgian architect.

Leuven University's 18th-century library at the Oude Markt was deliberately set alight by German troops during the First World War, rebuilt in a new location, and then severely damaged again during the Second World War. But this series of disasters had a silver lining, as behind its neo-Renaissance façade is a truly unique reading room designed by the Belgian architect Henry Lacoste in the 1940s. Fascinated by ancient civilisations and craftsmanship, the professor of archaeology and architecture channelled his many interests into a magnificent homage to wood. Light oak has been used to clad the 44m-long space in carved panels but also to create two levels of long galleries, an amazing sculpted clock, geometric balustrades, and stairs decorated with a lion and eagle fighting a snake. A display case shows remnants of burnt books, rare survivors from the 1914 fire, while stone walls are carved with the names of the international institutions who funded the library's reconstruction. A visit to the Library Tower includes an exhibition on the library's history. Visitors are only allowed in the main reading room during weekends and holidays.

bib.kuleuven.be/english +32 16 324 660

20 NATIONAL & UNIVERSITY LIBRARY OF SLOVENIA

Turjaška ulica 1, 1000 Ljubljana, Slovenia

TO VISIT BEFORE YOU DIE BECAUSE

Jože Plečnik's modernist masterpiece is a 'temple of knowledge' filled with original details and symbolic gestures, and built with the support of local students.

An unusual façade mixing red brick and stone, plus bronze doors with handles shaped like Pegasus' head – these are the first signs that this library is something quite special. Described as 'classical in character but with a modern twist' by architectural historian James Campbell, the National Library is considered Slovenian architect Jože Plečnik's finest work. It was built between 1936 and 1941 on the site of a baroque palace destroyed by an earthquake in 1895 (its remains provided some of the stones on the façade). To symbolise the ascent from the darkness of ignorance towards enlightenment, the library is accessed via a monumental central staircase with 32 pillars of black Podpeč marble. In contrast, its long reading room is brightly lit by two glass walls and a series of chandeliers designed, like all the furniture, by Plečnik himself. The desk legs are made of marble columns, and the railings from gas pipes. On weekdays visitors are only allowed in the entrance, staircase and exhibition room, so come on a Saturday afternoon to see the main reading room.

www.nuk.uni-lj.si +386 1 200 11 88

21 BRITISH LIBRARY

96 Euston Road, London NW1 2DB, UK

TO VISIT
BEFORE YOU DIE
BECAUSE

It took 36 years to build this landmark brick building for the national library of the UK, which holds a living collection that gets bigger every day.

Opened in 1998 on Euston Road, this brick behemoth designed by the architect Colin St John Wilson and his wife, MJ Long, is accessed via a courtyard with a sculpture of Isaac Newton by Eduardo Paolozzi. At its heart is a six-storey glass tower inspired by the Beinecke Rare Book Library (page 170), containing the King's Library with 65,000 printed volumes along with other pamphlets, manuscripts and maps. It's the largest public building constructed in the United Kingdom in the 20th century – yet it's still not big enough. A £1.1 billion extension is expected to start in 2026 and add about 9,200 sq m of extra library space and a full-height foyer. In the meantime, you can take a look at the *Magna Carta*, Geoffrey Chaucer's *Canterbury Tales* and Virginia Woolf's *Mrs Dalloway* in the wonderful Treasures galleries, or attend a temporary exhibition on themes such as maps or Harry Potter. After exploring the country's biggest library, head to nearby Charterhouse Square or Upper Street to visit some of its smallest: the red phone boxes here have been turned into free libraries. First started in Somerset in 2009, they can now be found all around the UK.

bl.uk +44 33 0333 1144

22 BRITISH MUSEUM READING ROOM

British Museum, Great Russell Street, London, WC1B 3DG, UK

TO VISIT BEFORE YOU DIE BECAUSE

A masterpiece of mid-19th-century technology at the heart of Norman Foster's covered courtyard, the Reading Room was once used by the country's great minds.

When the British Museum Library needed a larger reading room in the early 1850s, Antonio Panizzi, Keeper of Printed Books, suggested building a round room in the empty central courtyard. Inspired by the Pantheon in Rome, the design by Sydney Smirke used cast iron, concrete, glass and the latest heating and ventilation systems. More than 62,000 visitors came to marvel at the library when it opened in 1857. Under its 42m-diameter dome with a blue, cream and gold papier mâché ceiling once worked some of the greatest figures of the time, including Karl Marx, who wrote part of *Das Kapital* here; Lenin, who first asked for a reader's ticket in 1902; and novelists Bram Stoker, Arthur Conan Doyle and Virginia Woolf, who said she felt like 'a thought in the huge bald forehead which is so splendidly encircled by a band of famous names'. Playwright Edward Aveling wrote that this meeting place for radical thinkers was 'in equal degrees a menagerie and a lunatic asylum'. It contains 40km of shelves, but its books were moved to the new British Library (page 43) in 1997.

britishmuseum.org +44 20 7323 8000

23 ROYAL LIBRARY OF EL ESCORIAL

Avenida Juan de Borbón y Battenberg,
28200 San Lorenzo de El Escorial, Madrid, Spain

TO VISIT BEFORE YOU DIE BECAUSE

In a palace near Madrid, you will find this perfectly organised, immensely influential library – a statement of power, prowess and intellectual leadership.

Due to their cost and rarity, for centuries books were chained to the desks and lecterns of medieval libraries, their spine often hidden at the back and their fore edges exposed. But as volumes became more available and affordable, a new vision for the library emerged: a beautiful room with long walls lined with bookcases. The earliest and most impactful of these new libraries is the Escorial in Madrid, built by Juan Bautista de Toledo and Juan de Herrera in 1592 for King Philip II. Here, books are displayed the 'right' way around in tall bookcases decorated with marquetry and designed to fit in the grand scheme of the room, which became a model for monasteries and palaces all around Europe. The majestic 54m-long vaulted space comes with multicoloured frescoes by Pellegrino Tibaldi, and links the palace's monastery and the seminary. It holds 40,000 books, including 600 incunabulas and thousands of medieval codices. The further you go from the entrance, the more abstract the subject of the book, with theology, geometry and mathematics closest to the basilica.

el-escorial.com +34 918 905 902

24 MAFRA PALACE LIBRARY

Terreiro D. João V, 2640-492 Mafra, Portugal

TO VISIT BEFORE YOU DIE BECAUSE

An elegant vision in white, the world's longest Rococo library has been kept free of insects for centuries thanks to its colony of bats.

Said to contain over 150 staircases and 880 rooms, the vast Mafra Palace took decades to complete. By the time the workers finally started building its library, all grand plans for a rich, gilded interior had been abandoned. The resulting room, which is a staggering 88m long and 14m high, was completed in 1771 and simply whitewashed. Its distinct lack of colour and gold leaf makes it look particularly graceful to modern eyes and lets the Rococo carvings and intricate balustrades take centre stage. Hanging from the wood-panelled ceiling are original oil lamps, while visitors will have to use their imagination to fill the empty cartouches above the ornate bookcases, which hold around 36,000 leather-bound volumes dating from the 14th to the 19th centuries. They are kept safe from book-eating insects by a colony of bats that sleep behind the bookcases or in the garden. The only problem? The furniture needs to be completely covered every evening, and the floors swept every morning, to erase any evidence of bat poo. There are many other beautiful libraries to visit in nearby Lisbon, including São Lázaro, the city's oldest library, and the modernist Biblioteca Nacional.

palaciodemafra.pt +351 261 817 550

25 CHETHAM'S LIBRARY

Long Millgate, Manchester M3 1SB, UK

TO VISIT BEFORE YOU DIE BECAUSE

The oldest public library in the English-speaking world, it has welcomed readers including Charles Dickens, Daniel Defoe and Benjamin Franklin for over 350 years.

When he died in 1653, the wealthy Lancashire textile merchant Humphrey Chetham left a will that made provision for a school for 40 poor boys (now a specialist music school of world renown); for the creation of five chained libraries in local churches (the chains were a common feature to prevent theft in libraries up until the 18th century, when they were replaced by gated shelves); and for the opening of Chetham's Library. Housed in a magnificent 1421 sandstone building originally constructed as accommodation for a college of priests, its collection now comprises over 40 medieval manuscripts and 100,000 printed volumes, including a handful of books belonging to astrologer, alchemist and occultist John Dee, a warden at the college and the court astrologer for Elizabeth I. In the Reading Room, you can see one of the five chained libraries, the Gorton Chest, which contains moralising and religious works. It was in an alcove in that same room that Karl Marx and Friedrich Engels studied in the summer of 1845, ultimately leading to the publication of *The Communist Manifesto*. Access is via prebooked guided tours and events only; all proceeds go towards the upkeep of Chetham's Library, an independent charity.

library.chethams.com +44 161 834 7961

26 THE JOHN RYLANDS LIBRARY

150 Deansgate, Manchester M3 3EH, UK

TO VISIT BEFORE YOU DIE BECAUSE

One of Europe's finest examples of neo-Gothic architecture, this cathedral for books houses the special collections of the University of Manchester Library.

A gift to the city of Manchester, the John Rylands Library was purpose-built to give public access to world-class collections of rare books, manuscripts and archives. Although it is named after local textile magnate and philanthropist John Rylands, it is actually his wife Enriqueta who was instrumental in the library's opening in 1900. She bought entire collections – 40,000 books and rarities from the 2nd Earl Spencer and 6,000 manuscripts from the 26th Earl of Crawford – and commissioned the architect Basil Champneys to build an imposing building in honour of her beloved husband. She seemed to have been quite a character, going against her architect's wishes to select decorations and statues for her library. Recently reopened after a complete upgrade, the exhibition spaces showcase precious items from the Rylands' vast collections, which might include Papyrus P52, perhaps the earliest extant New Testament text; a Gutenberg Bible; a collection of printing by William Caxton; and the personal papers of novelist Elizabeth Gaskell and scientist John Dalton.

library.manchester.ac.uk/rylands

27 JESUIT LIBRARY AT MARIA LAACH ABBEY

Benedictine Abbey of Maria Laach, 56653, Germany

TO VISIT BEFORE YOU DIE BECAUSE

Located in a beautiful, working Benedictine abbey just south of Bonn, this 19th-century library is still used by monks for study and research.

Given the vagaries of time, it's a miracle that there are any libraries – or indeed any books – left today. This is certainly the case at the Benedictine Abbey of Maria Laach. Founded in 1093, its scriptorium was once full of monks expertly copying precious manuscripts. All was lost when the abbey was dissolved in 1802, but luckily, a new library was built in 1862 by the Jesuits, who moved in briefly, before being expelled from the German Empire in 1872. They took all their books with them as they left, of course, which meant the new occupiers – the Benedictines once again – had to refill the library with books. They found only two of the original manuscripts from the medieval library but acquired many more and ran out of space pretty quickly. The room, with its gorgeous wooden steps and galleries, and central spiral staircase soaring towards the white ceiling and skylight, is completely packed with books. A new library archive was built nearby in 2013 to house the rest of the 275,000 volumes. To visit, join one of the guided tours on Sunday afternoons.

maria-laach.de/bibliothek +49 265 259 350

28 RUSSIAN STATE LIBRARY

Vozdvizhenka Street, 3/5, Moscow 119019, Russia

TO VISIT BEFORE YOU DIE BECAUSE

One of the largest libraries in the world, the Russian State Library boasts a fascinating history and a striking modernist extension guarded by the bust of Lenin.

Libraries have always been political spaces; their collections are shaped by the concerns of the time, and the will of those in power. The Russian State Library, for example, was reorganised after the Russian Revolution of 1917 under the leadership of Vladimir I. Lenin (the library's local nickname is Leninka). The Soviet leader viewed libraries as crucial for the education of the working class and for propagating socialist ideology. There's a fine line between propaganda and censorship, and Lenin's successors, from Stalin to Putin, have banned many books (LGBTQ+ content is as unlikely to be found here as in a school library in Florida). The library's collection, which includes the contents of confiscated private libraries and the Rumyantsev Museum collection, is spread between the 18th-century Pashkov House and the stark but beautiful 1940s Lenin Library building, whose central staircase was inspired by Friedrich von Gärtner's Bayerische Staatsbibliothek (like those of the Stockholm and Ljubljana libraries, pages 70 and 42). In the biggest of the library's 36 reading rooms, the bust of Lenin still watches over readers today.

+7 800 100 57 90

29 DEICHMAN BJØRVIKA

Anne-Cath, Vestlys plass 1, 0150 Oslo, Norway

TO VISIT BEFORE YOU DIE BECAUSE

Winner of the 2021 IFLA Public Library of the Year Award, Oslo's main library seamlessly connects with its surroundings and offers high-tech facilities to all.

Located next to the Oslo Opera House and Munch Museum on Oslo's waterfront, Deichman Bjørvika was designed as a welcoming, inclusive space. It opened in June 2020, in the middle of the Covid pandemic, and was an instant success even then. 'The librarians wanted a house that would inspire visitors to explore all the new facilities and activities the modern library can offer,' explain its architects Atelier Oslo and Lundhagem. 'This motivated us to create an open and intriguing building in which you are constantly invited around the next corner, to discover new places.' There are three entrances and three atriums distributing light throughout the building, whose top floor cantilevers above a public square. The basement includes a cinema and a 180-seat venue, while the top floors feature quieter spaces for study and reflection. There are also recording studios, a makerspace and a natural sciences section with a wall of living plants. A new system means library cards are not needed, and allows librarians to create digital recommendations of books and other items, which can be displayed on interactive screens on the library's shelves.

deichman.no/bibliotekene/bjørvika +47 23 43 29 00

30 BODLEIAN LIBRARY

Broad Street, Oxford OX1 3BG, UK

TO VISIT BEFORE YOU DIE BECAUSE

Dating back to 1488, 'the Bod' has welcomed generations of scholars, Nobel Prize winners and writers, including Oscar Wilde, C.S. Lewis and J.R.R. Tolkien.

Named after Thomas Bodley, who raised funds to re-establish the university library in Oxford after the Reformation, this collection of libraries in the heart of Oxford is arranged around the medieval Duke Humfrey's Library, now part of a striking Gothic courtyard known as Old Schools Quadrangle. Opened in 1602, Bodley's extension features beautifully painted panels, caged staircases and wooden columns linking benches with galleries above. It can be visited as part of a tour starting just below, in the Divinity School, under an elaborately carved fan-vaulted ceiling. The guided visits also take in Convocation House (the university's 'parliament house'), Chancellor's Court (an oak-panelled courtroom) and the iconic 18th-century Radcliffe Camera. Britain's first circular library, it is named after its benefactor, the royal physician John Radcliffe, and since 2011 accessed via the Gladstone Link, an underground library. On the other side of the quadrangle is Hawksmoor's Clarendon Building (now office spaces) and the Weston Library, home to an exhibition showcasing its treasures, from the sumptuously illuminated *Romance of Alexander* to the manuscripts of Jane Austen.

visit.bodleian.ox.ac.uk +44 1865 287 400

31 BNF FRANÇOIS-MITTERRAND

Quai François Mauriac, 75706 Paris, France

TO VISIT
BEFORE YOU DIE
BECAUSE

This minimalist building takes the books out of the basement and into four towers surrounding light-filled reading rooms and a peaceful sunken garden.

In the 1980s, French president François Mitterrand put his mark on the capital with a series of 'Grands Projets', an ambitious cultural and architectural initiative that saw the opening of new landmarks such as the Louvre Pyramid, the Opéra Bastille and this contemporary library, built on a stretch of industrial wasteland on the banks of the Seine. 'The greatest gift that it is possible to give to Paris consists, today, in offering space, and emptiness – in a word, a place that is open, free and stirring,' wrote its architect Dominique Perrault. Space is indeed a luxury here, and instead of filling the site with a flashy building, he has mirrored the Concorde, Champ de Mars and Invalides esplanades to create both a 'square for Paris' and 'a library for France'. At each corner are four towers, shaped like open books facing one another. These beacons of knowledge are filled with the Bibliothèque de France's precious collections and surrounded by a huge wooden deck. Cosy reading rooms overlook the peaceful sunken garden at the heart of the site, while the Hall des Globes showcases giant twin globes of the earth and the heavens made for Louis XIV. There's a wonderful programme of exhibitions, on themes such as photography, prints or comics.

bnf.fr/fr/francois-mitterrand

+33 153 795 959

32 BNF RICHELIEU

5 rue Vivienne, 75002 Paris, France

TO VISIT
BEFORE YOU DIE
BECAUSE

The main branch of France's national library is a magnet for art lovers, with a museum, galleries, gardens and a magnificent reading room filled with comics.

This former cardinal's palace is the historic site of the Bibliothèque Nationale de France (now spread over five sites, including the BNF François-Mitterrand, page 55). The institution holds over 40 million documents collected over five centuries, but here at Richelieu the focus is on performing arts, maps, prints and photography, music, coins, medals and antiquities. Some of these gems are on display at the library's recently refurbished museum and popular temporary exhibitions. The palace is beautiful, but the adjoining reading rooms are truly spectacular. Salle Labrouste is a 1860s masterpiece with glazed cupolas and leafy murals but is accessible to the general public only on special occasions (you can visit another Labrouste library, Sainte-Geneviève, page 58). However, the second space, Salle Ovale, is open to all, including children, and free to enter. Completed in 1932 and designed by Jean-Louis Pascal, it boasts an 18m-high ceiling with a skylight surrounded by mosaics and floral decorations. It is known for its collection of 9,000 comics, ranging from *bandes dessinées* to manga, and from Rodolphe Töpffer's 1830 comic strips to the latest *Astérix*.

bnf.fr/fr/richelieu +33 153 795 959

33 SAINTE-GENEVIÈVE LIBRARY

10 place du Panthéon, 75005 Paris, France

TO VISIT
BEFORE YOU DIE
BECAUSE

Opened in 1851, the capital's first purpose-built library is a fantastic space with cast-iron arches and colourful murals just opposite the Panthéon.

Like Berlin and Toronto, Paris is a hotspot for beautiful libraries. As well as the BNF branches, there are the Bibliothèque Mazarine, France's oldest public library; the Bibliothèque Forney, in the 15th-century Hôtel de Sens; the Bibliothèque de l'Assemblée Nationale, with a ceiling by Eugène Delacroix; and the wood-panelled Bibliothèque de l'Hôtel de Ville. But perhaps the most Parisian of all is Bibliothèque Sainte-Geneviève in the Latin Quarter. Artist Marcel Duchamp once worked as a librarian here, while famous readers include Simone de Beauvoir. An entrance lobby decorated with garden murals and marble busts leads to the 80m-long first-floor reading room. There, 60 years before the construction of the Eiffel Tower, renowned architect Henri Labrouste created a fabulous cast-iron roof, two rows of arches supported by 16 columns raised on stone plinths. The library was lit by gas lamps, and metal was chosen over wood due to fire risk. Its symmetrical façade is engraved with the names of scholars and writers, and has been copied around the world, for example at the Boston Public Library. The library is home to 2 million documents, including an extensive Nordic library.

bsg.univ-paris3.fr +33 144 419 797

34 L'ANIMU

Voie romaine, 20137 Porto-Vecchio, Corsica, France

TO VISIT
BEFORE YOU DIE
BECAUSE

Nesled amond olive trees, this building by Dominique Coulon & Associés symbolises the importance of the local public library in France.

Since the 1980s, France has had an ambitious programme for its 15,500 public libraries, doubling the numbers of users and of documents available, transforming former hospitals and theatres into new cultural hubs, and building contemporary 'médiathèques'. A perfect example can be found here in the south of Corsica, in a building opened in 2021 – the same year that French law defined the library as an 'essential public service' guaranteeing access to culture and information to all citizens. Surrounded by oak and olive trees, the media library was designed by Dominique Coulon & Associés to complement the landscape. It appears to float lightly above ground, its shape informed by the location of every tree and rock on the site, which also includes a garden, shaded terrace and summer bar. Inside there are spaces for meetings and workshops and two reading areas (for children and grown-ups). L'Animu's logo is inspired by the pifanu seashell, an ancient wind instrument, while its 21,000 items include a large Corsican section. The team here organise over 260 events every year and have recently opened a *ludothèque* (toy and board game library).

animu.corsica +33 495 233 589

35 NATIONAL LIBRARY OF THE CZECH REPUBLIC

Mariánské nám. 190/5, 110 00 Praha 1, Czech Republic

TO VISIT BEFORE YOU DIE BECAUSE

Boasting a Baroque Library and Astronomical Tower, this historic scientific hub visited by Mozart is turned towards the skies and stars.

A former Jesuit college completed in 1726, the Klementinum is a large complex of baroque buildings in the heart of Prague's Old Town. In its vine-covered courtyard you will find the National Library of the Czech Republic, as well as a large collection of sundials. It has been a centre for scientific knowledge for centuries, its collection including astronomer Johannes Kepler's annotated writings, as well as important medieval manuscripts. Guided tours take visitors to the entrance of the Baroque Library Hall. Home to a series of antique globes and books published before 1801, it has a gorgeous ceiling fresco by Jan Hiebl depicting human knowledge. After marvelling at reproductions of the 17th-century sextants used by Tycho Brahe in the ante-room, climb the Astronomical Tower for great views to the castle. Meteorological data has been collected from here since Josef Stepling introduced the idea in 1775. The library also holds the letters and music of Mozart, who visited the library in 1787 with his wife Constanze while playing in Prague for the first time.

nkp.cz/en +420 221 663 275

36 NATIONAL LIBRARY OF KOSOVO

Sheshi 'Hasan Prishtina' p.n, Pristina 10000, Kosovo

TO VISIT BEFORE YOU DIE BECAUSE

This one-of-a-kind library blends Byzantine and Islamic architectural forms to create a highly detailed brutalist building, lit by dozens of plexiglass domes.

The ugliest building ever, or a stroke of genius encapsulating the local vernacular in a modern, brutalist form? Up to you to decide what to make of this 1982 library by Croatian architect Andrija Mutnjaković. Named after 17th-century writer Pjetër Bogdani, the father of Albanian prose, it is wrapped in a metal net and lit by 74 domes, inspired by the shape of Kosovo's national hat, or perhaps by the domes of the Turkish baths in Prizren and the Serbian Orthodox monastery of Peć. Inside there are wall mosaics, a rectangular oak balustrade and circular decorations inspired by Bronze Age Illyrian fibulae. The building's history is also dramatic: during the Yugoslav Wars, it was used as a command-and-control centre by the Yugoslav Army, who smashed the furniture and dumped the card catalogue in the basement; some 100,000 Albanian-language books are thought to have been pulped. To see the building in all its glory, head to the Cathedral of Saint Mother Teresa, where you can take a lift up to the top of the tower for a great shot of the library and 360-degree views of the city.

biblioteka-ks.org +381 38 212 416

37 PICCOLOMINI LIBRARY

Piazza Duomo 8, 53100 Siena, Italy

TO VISIT
BEFORE YOU DIE
BECAUSE

Visiting this dazzling example of Italian Gothic architecture with Renaissance frescoes is like stepping into a manuscript's colourful illuminations.

This library has just one room, and only a handful of books. But what a room, and what books! You will find it in the medieval Siena Cathedral, whose eye-catching black-and-white marble stripes reference the Tuscan city's coat of arms. Built by Pope Pius III in around 1492 to honour his uncle Aeneas Silvius Piccolomini (better known as Pope Pius II), it was meant to house Piccolomini's rich collection of books, rare parchments and manuscripts. Most have been lost, but on display in the library today are a series of illuminated codices (graduals and antiphonaries), a collection offering an almost complete overview of the history of Italian illumination in the 15th century, with works by famous illustrators Girolamo da Cremona and Liberale da Verona. The colourful manuscripts are matched by the room itself, resplendent with a blue ceramic floor decorated with crescent moons (part of the Piccolomini emblem) and bright, colourful frescoes on all its walls and ceiling. Painted by Pinturicchio between 1503 and 1508, they celebrate the life and work of Pius II.

operaduomo.siena.it/libreria-piccolomini +39 577 286 300

38 SPIJKENISSE PUBLIC LIBRARY

Markt 40, 3201CZ Spijkenisse, The Netherlands

TO VISIT BEFORE YOU DIE BECAUSE

A monument to the power and pleasure of reading, this 'Book Mountain' takes pride of place in the town's market square.

Visible for miles, this library is both an advertisement and an invitation for reading, in a community with a 10 per cent illiteracy rate. MVRDV, the Dutch architecture practice also responsible for the Tianjin Binhai Library (page 131), have stacked all the different spaces needed for the library (education centre, a chess club, auditorium, meeting rooms, commercial offices and retail space) into a pyramid. You can follow a winding path up 480 m-long brick staircases to its five floors of terraces and reading rooms, following a book trail that culminates at the top of the pyramid. The whole library is wrapped in a glass structure shaped like a giant traditional Dutch farmhouse, complete with pitched roof and brick chimney. The space is filled with plants and is a benchmark for sustainable technologies. The energy-efficient building uses natural ventilation and recycles rainwater for its toilets and underfloor heating and cooling of the library space. In nearby Rotterdam, the Central Library, designed in 1977 by Van den Broek & Bakema and known for its giant yellow tubes, is currently being renovated.

bibliotheekzhe.nl +31 88 006 7500

39 ST. GALLEN'S ABBEY LIBRARY

Klosterhof 6d, 9000 St. Gallen, Switzerland

TO VISIT BEFORE YOU DIE BECAUSE

This UNESCO World Heritage site and Memory of the World collection preserves key specimens of European intellectual history in a jaw-dropping Baroque Hall.

On the doorway of St. Gallen's Abbey Library, made in 1781 by Franz Anton Dirr, is a Greek inscription: 'Psyches Iatreion', or 'healing-place of the soul' – a description that most bibliophiles would agree with when they enter the Baroque Hall. Completed in 1767, the spectacular space is wrapped in swirling galleries, with a busy Rococo ceiling and trompe l'œil scenes. Unlike at Admont (page 16) where the woodwork is painted white, here the bookcases and columns (some of which open to reveal finding lists) are made of shiny polished wood. The exquisite joinery extends to the patterned fir wood floor (visitors have to wear slippers to protect it). But the abbey's literary treasures are much older than this room; the valuable collection goes back practically without interruption more than 1,300 years, to the time when the abbey was originally founded by Irish missionaries Gall and Otmar. It includes a corpus of early medieval manuscripts, mostly produced in the abbey's scriptorium, as well as a Wunderkammer and a Great Globe. Some are on show in the room and in a separate temporary exhibition gallery.

 stiftsbezirk.ch/en/stiftsbibliothek +41 71 227 34 16

40 CITY OF STOCKHOLM LIBRARY

Odengatan 53, 113 50 Stockholm, Sweden

TO VISIT
BEFORE YOU DIE
BECAUSE

Gunnar Asplund's masterpiece blends monumental doorways, Egyptian friezes and bespoke finishings to create a modernist temple to literature.

In 1918, the City of Stockholm Library sent architect Gunnar Asplund around the world to research libraries and prepare a brief for a competition. His report was so good that they hired him instantly to design their new building and adjoining park. Completed in 1928, the library is an instantly recognisable bright-orange square volume topped with a cylinder, said to have been inspired by the maverick French architect Claude-Nicolas Ledoux's highly unusual geometric creations. Past the huge doorway, the black walls of the entrance hall are decorated with scenes from the *Iliad*. A monumental dark staircase leads to a large circular reading room with tall white walls that reflect light into the space – a truly inspiring contrast. 'Since I was a kid, I have always felt I was entering a church when ascending the stairs of the main library,' says librarian Einar Ehn-Briem. 'After more than 10 years as a librarian and 44 years on earth, that feeling remains.' With its 24m-high ceiling and cloud-like ring of stucco wall, it's certainly a heavenly space. The library is closed for refurbishment until 2027, so in the meantime, visit the National Library of Sweden.

biblioteket.stockholm.se

Hc·Hce SKÖNLITTERATUR
TILL GALLERI 2

41 STUTTGART CITY LIBRARY

Mailänder Platz 1, 70173 Stuttgart, Germany

TO VISIT BEFORE YOU DIE BECAUSE

This ultra-modern white cube looks beautiful inside and out, but is also a welcoming, practical public library that celebrates local culture and the art of animation.

Glowing blue at night, this cubical library sits proudly on a plot reclaimed from railways in Stuttgart's Europaviertel neighbourhood. Inspired by the Bauhaus' love for geometry, the 45m monolith, with a 9x9 grid of windows, has become one of the city's top attractions since its opening in 2011. Its architect, Eun Young Yi, chose pearl-grey concrete and frosted glass bricks for its façade, but it is the interiors that really impress. Stepping inside, you will be forgiven for wondering where the books are: the entrance, a cube within a cube, is a large void illuminated by a central roof light and designed as a meditative area. Above it is the main reading room, an atrium flooded with light and spreading over five levels of galleries. There are over 2 million items to choose from, including an entire floor dedicated to children, another to music, and the Online Animation Library, one of the largest repositories of contemporary animated film in the world. Locals love the cosy nooks hidden among the shelves, the top-floor café and the rooftop terrace. On the ground floor you can borrow audio guides to tour the building, and visit an exhibition showcasing local authors.

stadtbibliothek-stuttgart.de +49 711 21 691 100

42 HANDELINGENKAMER

Het Binnenhof, 2511 CL Den Haag, The Netherlands

TO VISIT BEFORE YOU DIE BECAUSE

The red-and-green library of the Dutch House of Representatives has unique decorations inspired by Chinese dragons.

Inside The Hague's former Department of Justice, a 1876 neo-Renaissance building by Cornelis Hendrik Peters, is the Proceedings Room, built to store the verbatim reports (Handelingen in Dutch) of all the debates in the House of Representatives. At first glance, its cast-iron balustrades, stained-glass roof and spiral staircases look as flowery and flamboyant as you'd expect for the time. But look closely and you will notice that Peters incorporated many Chinese influences into the design, adding dragon heads to the railings, handles in the shape of dragon claws, and scales on the skylight. The 9m-high space can accommodate up to 30,000 volumes (two centuries' worth of reports) – although the 1940–1945 section has been left empty, as a reminder that parliament did not meet during the German occupation. The library is only open to visitors during special events such as Dag van de Bouw or Open Monument Day. As the parliament buildings are currently being renovated, these visits are not guaranteed. For another library in a similar style, head to Amsterdam's Rijksmuseum, where the Cuypers Library, designed by Peters' teacher Pierre Cuypers, can be seen from a viewing balcony in room 2.16.

dagvandebouw.nl openmonumentendag.nl

43 LOCHAL

Burgemeester Brokxlaan 1000, 5041 SG Tilburg,
The Netherlands

TO VISIT
BEFORE YOU DIE
BECAUSE

Housed in a former locomotive hall and featuring bookshop-like displays, this flexible cultural hub celebrates the city's industrial heritage.

Tilburg's state-of-the-art LocHal was opened in 2019 in a workshop building on a former railway marshalling yard. The then-empty 1932 locomotive hall was reconfigured by a team of architects into a covered city square with a library, a cafe, an exhibition area and office spaces for cultural organisations. 'We want to connect people, facilitate interaction and the sharing of knowledge and stories in order to make a difference,' writes its former director Peter Kok. Under the 18m-high ceilings are workshops and meeting spaces with flexible wooden seating elements, and six huge, locally made textile curtains that can be moved around to create different 'rooms' or soften the light flowing in from the glass façade. A performance stage is built out of stacks of old books topped with an oak platform, steps double up as an auditorium, and three 'train tables' can be moved on the original tracks to create a catwalk. There are six labs dedicated to local history, new media, games, food, creative writing and citizen projects, while the children's library is inspired by the famous local theme park Efteling and colouring pencils.

lochal.nl/en +31 13 464 8500

44 WIBLINGEN ABBEY LIBRARY

Schloßstraße 38, 89079 Ulm, Germany

TO VISIT BEFORE YOU DIE BECAUSE

This heavenly pastel Rococo library is decorated with a fresco by renowned painter Franz Martin Kuen depicting divine wisdom.

In the 18th century, medieval monasteries all around central Europe started building magnificent baroque libraries to house their collections, trying to outdo each other with the prettiest putti, glitziest gold leaf and most inspiring frescoes. From Admont (page 16) to St. Gallen (page 67), but also Melk, Altenburg, St Florian, Strahov or Waldsassen, these building projects boosted the economy and provided suitably majestic facilities for the visiting abbots and emperor. At Wiblingen near Ulm, the spectacular library takes over the central part of the north wing of the abbey, with a gorgeous pastel palette and a curved gallerie. It's full of visual tricks: the columns and statues appear to be made of shiny marble but are in fact painted wood, while bookcases on wheels slide to reveal doorways in the gallery. Behind the style there was substance: monasteries were islands of learning and Wiblingen was part of the Melk Reform, a movement promoting learning and humanism in the area (fittingly, it now houses the University of Ulm's Academy for Health Professions).

 kloster-wiblingen.de +49 731 27 013 500

45 UTRECHT NEUDE LIBRARY

Neude 11, 3512 TA Utrecht, The Netherlands

TO VISIT BEFORE YOU DIE BECAUSE

Located in an iconic listed brick building, it's a suitably impressive library for a UNESCO City of Literature once home to Descartes, Locke and Hegel.

Standing under the parabolic brick arches in the main hall of this wonderful building in central Utrecht, you would never guess what its original purpose was. Its scale and stained glass point towards a religious building of some sort, while its large clock indicates it might have been a train station. In fact, it was built as the city's main post office – the 'Temple for Post and Telegraphy' – in 1924 by Joseph Crouwel, in what is known as the Amsterdam School style. Since 2020 it has been home to the main branch of Utrecht's public library, its black art deco statues representing the continents now watching over new generations of readers. It's a hive of activity offering craft workshops, a language café and cultural events, where locals pop in to borrow a cookbook or get help with their digital skills. The library also highlights the work of local creatives, with a neon light artwork by Maarten Baas above the entrance and a statue of Miffy, the beloved little rabbit created by Utrecht-born Dick Bruna, in the children's library.

bibliotheekutrecht.nl +31 30 286 1800

46 MARCIANA LIBRARY

Piazzetta San Marco, 7, 30124 Venezia, Italy

TO VISIT BEFORE YOU DIE BECAUSE

One of Italy's most important research libraries, the Marciana is located in a 16th-century building near Venice's St Mark's Square and Doge's Palace.

Before his death in 1472, Cardinal Basilios Bessarion had agreed to donate his fine collection of Greek manuscripts to the Venetian state, providing that they were made available to everyone. But they stayed in their wooden crates until finally a suitable home was built for them in the heart of the city in the 1580s. The great architect Jacopo Sansovino designed a sumptuous building, renowned for its intricate columned façade, with a grand staircase leading up to a library with a balcony overlooking St Mark's Square. There is a Titian ceiling and classical sculptures from the Grimani collection in the vestibule, while the long reading room features ceiling roundels by the leading Venetian artists of the time, including Veronese. Incredibly, the first ceiling built by Sansovino collapsed, and he was sent to prison, before having to pay for the new one out of his own pocket. Display cases now stand where rows of wooden lecterns and chained books once awaited readers (the Malatestiana Moderna in Cesena still has them). The other great Italian library, the Laurentian Library in Florence designed by Michelangelo, is equally incredible but more difficult to visit.

bibliotecanazionalemarciana.cultura.gov.it +39 041 240 7211

47 CAPITOLARE LIBRARY

Piazza Duomo 19, 37121 Verona, Italy

TO VISIT
BEFORE YOU DIE
BECAUSE

Follow in the footsteps of Dante and Petrarca to this former medieval scriptorium, the world's oldest continually active independent library.

The Biblioteca Capitolare started off as a scriptorium, a prolific book-making workshop in the shadow of the cathedral of Verona, where one day a clerk called Ursicinus signed the manuscript he had just finished copying and marked it with the date, 1 August 517. Some centuries later, it became a place of study visited by the likes of Dante Alighieri and Francesco Petrarca. Amassed over 1,500 years, the Capitolare's collection includes 100,000 books – among them 1,280 manuscripts and 250 incunabula – as well as 11,000 parchments. Highlights range from one of the oldest surviving purple Gospels and the world's oldest copy of St Augustine's *De Civitate Dei*, produced when its author was still alive, to the famous Veronese Riddle, a short puzzle that is the first written occurrence of the Italian language, and to the oldest known representation of the city of Verona. Now a non-profit organisation, the library offers guided tours and events and opened a museum in 2023. There you can admire the historic cloister and marvel at some of its literary treasures to the sound of Gregorian chants.

bibliotecacapitolare.it +39 33 15 946 961

48 AUSTRIAN NATIONAL LIBRARY

Josefsplatz 1, 1015 Vienna, Austria

TO VISIT BEFORE YOU DIE BECAUSE

Founded by the Habsburgs, this palatial building boasts the largest Rococo library ever built, as well as four special museums.

Opened in 1730 on Vienna's then-new Josefsplatz, the extravagant State Hall of the Austrian National library was created for Charles VI by Johann Bernhard Fischer von Erlach, one of the leading architects and stage-set designers of his day. As a court library, it was open to all and built to impress. The star of the show here is the building rather than the 200,000 books, which look tiny surrounded by the oversized columns. Visitors feel like Lilliputians under the 20m-high ceilings, with a central fresco representing the emperor in all his glory, holding a pyramid and laurel wreath. Treasures on display in the hall include a pair of Venetian globes; you can see more in the library's Globe Museum, the only of its kind in the world. There are also the Papyrus Museum, which holds artefacts more than 3,000 years old; the Esperanto Museum; and the Literature Museum. The library's 19 reading rooms are all open to the public. For something completely different, Vienna is also home to a futuristic university library designed by Zaha Hadid.

onb.ac.at/en +43 153 410

49 DEPETRUS

Heuvel 2, 5261 EE Vught, The Netherlands

TO VISIT BEFORE YOU DIE BECAUSE

This former church was resurrected into a state-of-the-art, instantly popular cultural hub thanks to the initiative of local citizens.

When it was built in 1881, no one from the congregation of Saint Peter could have guessed that just over 135 years later, the neo-Romanesque church would narrowly escape demolition to become the city's public library. In 2011, a handful of local entrepreneurs joined forces to take over the building, renovating its exterior with the help of various grants before reopening it in 2019 as a community hub for the small town. Architect Jan David Hanrath has designed a flexible space where all functions (library, museum, meeting space, boutique, workspaces, welfare organisation and café) intermingle. The library's bookshelves are placed on rails so that they can be moved to the side when the space hosts large events or concerts, while the striking mezzanine runs both inside and outside the church, where it forms an entrance canopy. 'My favourite aspect of this library is the toy cabinet,' says librarian Henriëtte van Lamoen. 'For me, it contains a beautiful collection, in which the focus areas of my work as a community librarian come together. This is a fantastic space to work in.'

depetrus.nl

50 UB LAW

Rämistrasse 74, 8001 Zurich, Switzerland

TO VISIT BEFORE YOU DIE BECAUSE

Capped by a glass dome, this stunning curved wooden atrium library is embedded in a historic building remodelled by Santiago Calatrava.

Spanish-Swiss architect Santiago Calatrava is known for his futuristic white buildings with elegant wings that soar into the sky, but here in his adopted town of Zurich, he was constrained by a narrow, urban site – the courtyard of the University of Zurich's former chemistry building, dating from 1909. Instead of filling it with new floors, he offered instead to slot a new library for the Institute of Law into the space while maintaining an airy atrium at its heart. Opened in 2004, the library comes with six oval rings that seem to float around the original building. They are made of maple wood, with long desks built into the parapets, and help absorb sound to keep the library quiet. The collection includes approximately 230,000 books and 600 periodicals, all arranged around this new atrium. High-tech touches include a hydraulic pleated curtain of collapsible blades that controls the amount of natural light flowing from the skylight into the reading room. Meanwhile, the domed copper roof is inspired by surrounding cupolas. The library can be visited by individuals and smaller groups (up to five people) during opening hours without booking.

ub.uzh.ch +41 44 634 3099

51 NAKAJIMA LIBRARY

Okutsubakidaii-193-2 Yuwa Tsubakigawa, Akita 010-1292, Japan

TO VISIT BEFORE YOU DIE BECAUSE

The only library in Japan that is open around the clock, this peaceful space celebrates the beauty and strength of Akita cedar.

Named after Akita International University's founder, Mineo Nakajima, this award-winning library was designed by architect Mitsuru Senda using Akita's most famous material, cedar. It grows tall and straight in the mountainous region, where it is used to craft everything from delicate lunchboxes to sturdy canoes. Here, Senda has harnessed traditional timber-building techniques to create a parasol-shaped roof that unfurls above a semicircular reading room. The result is a 'book coliseum' and 'arena of knowledge' where students can read, meet and work 24 hours a day, 7 days a week (the library is open from 10am to 5pm for the general public). The inspiring setting is home to 86,446 books, curved bookshelves and disc-shaped lamps that appear to hover above the beautifully crafted wooden tables. It has a collection that includes about 60 per cent of books in foreign languages as well as a wealth of digital resources. Senda's Ishikawa Prefectural Library in Kanazawa is also worth a visit if you are in the area.

web.aiu.ac.jp/en/education/support/library/outline

52 CAMEL LIBRARY

Remote and rural areas of Balochistan, Pakistan

TO VISIT BEFORE YOU DIE BECAUSE

This camel-powered travelling library brings books – and thus hope, joy and knowledge – to the children living in the deserts of south-western Pakistan.

Travelling libraries take the form of *bibliobus* or 'library on wheels' in Europe and North America, *biblioburro* (donkey library) in Colombia and *perahu pustaka* (book boat) in Indonesia. Here in rural Pakistan, books are brought to their readers by camel, thanks to the Alif Laila Book Bus Society. Since 2021, the local NGO has been sharing the joy of reading with over 2,500 children. The camel comes laden with colourful boxes filled with books in local languages, while the travelling librarian offers storytelling sessions attended by whole villages, turning reading into a celebration. 'I used to be just a guide,' says volunteer Akhtar Baloch. 'Now, I'm a storyteller. Children in every village wait for me. This is the most beautiful journey of my life.' The enthusiasm is shared by young readers like Shazia, 9, from Chagai: 'When the book camel comes, we all run to it! Every time there are new colours, new characters, new dreams.' Helping children develop critical literacy skills one story at a time, this inspiring project has given hope to parents for a better future for their children.

aliflaila.org.pk

53 CHULALONGKORN UNIVERSITY LIBRARY

254 Phayathai Road, Wang Mai, Pathum Wan District, Bangkok 10330, Thailand

TO VISIT BEFORE YOU DIE BECAUSE

This experimental take on the physical space that is a library is an inspiring maze of possibilities and creativity for architecture students.

This library was created by Bangkok practice Department of Architecture as a reflection on the new possibilities in library design in an increasingly digital world. Completed in 2019, their reimagining of the concept hopes to reactivate the traditional learning space into a 1,260 sq m 'creative incubator' for students of architecture. Most striking is the 3D-grid system enveloping the co-working space, which, along with magnetic pin boards and digital screens, can be used by students as they wish, for example to display items or create exhibitions. The space also includes an occasional lecture/reading space with pixelated steps, and offers digital media and movies as well as physical books. The latter are often displayed with their covers facing out, rather than the usual line of spines, in order to invite people to pick them up and read them. 'Carrels are rearranged in a labyrinth configuration to minimise disturbance from the circulation around, while the reflective ceiling reveals the plan of the luminous maze,' explain the architects. The library is only open to visitors on Saturdays; please make sure to bring a valid ID for entry.

chula.ac.th +66 2218 4302

SPRING
Esquire
Esquire
MANUSYA
MANUSYA
MANUSYA
Go make it. We'll protect it.

COLOR SPACE

54 BEIJING LIBRARY

Urban Green Heart Forest Park, Tongzhou District, Beijing, China

TO VISIT BEFORE YOU DIE BECAUSE

This glass-lined library by Snøhetta boasts the world's largest reading space, a forest of soaring ginkgo columns and a valley of books.

A new landmark in Beijing's eastern Tongzhou District, this multi-award-winning project – dubbed IFLA Public Library of the Year 2024 – is the world's largest climatised reading space and China's largest load-bearing glass system. Its immense size is matched by superlative design by pioneering Norwegian studio Snøhetta, whose team aimed to reinstate the relevance of libraries in the digital age, making 'the open exchange of ideas and human dialogue its core purpose'. At the heart of the 75,000 sq m library is a sweeping 16m-tall forum with stepped, curved terraces that sculpt a central meandering path mirroring the course of the nearby Tonghui River. Dotted with columns that mushroom into ginkgo leaf-inspired panels, this magical interior landscape comes with semi-private reading areas as well as dedicated spaces for exhibitions, performances, conferences and the restoration of ancient books – all hidden in the 'hillsides'. Although warm, welcoming and connected to the surrounding nature, this is a high-tech project with the highest attainable sustainability standard in the country and one of the largest automated book storage systems in the world.

bjlib.clcn.net.cn +86 10 6735 8114 2103

55 NATIONAL LIBRARY OF CHINA

No. 33 Zhongguancun South Main Street, Haidian District, Beijing 100081, China

TO VISIT BEFORE YOU DIE BECAUSE

It's the largest library in Asia, with more than 41 million items plus exhibition rooms in its light-filled contemporary North Complex.

German architects KSP Engel & Zimmermann decided to go against the grain, designing the National Library of China as a horizontal building to complement the capital's forest of high-rises, which were rising at an incredible speed when the library was completed in 2008. An 80,000 sq m extension of a listed building, their new North Complex library houses over 12 million books and 2,000 reading seats in a structure comprising a podium, transparent hall and 'floating' roof home to the digital library. 'The three sections represent past, present and future and thus form a temporal axis of cultural heritage,' write the architects. Visible from all directions, the collection is housed in a glass shrine at the base of the building. Head up to the gallery to take in the vast square reading room, a true well of knowledge, before exploring the exhibition halls. There you will find some archaeological treasures, ancient manuscripts and block-printed volumes, as well as interactive screens (most explanations are in Chinese). Like most other national libraries, the NLC is also home to an excellent boutique offering high-end art and souvenirs.

www.nlc.cn

+86 10 8854 4114

56 CLOUD CAVE LIBRARY

Century Park, Shiji, Longhua District, Haikou, Hainan 570228, China

TO VISIT BEFORE YOU DIE BECAUSE

Part of the redevelopment of Haikou's coastline, this library with smooth white concrete curves was designed as a portal into another dimension.

Just like the best book transports readers away from everyday reality, this sculptural library completed in 2021 by MAD Architects aims to offer a surreal experience to visitors – 'a journey transcending time and space', hence its nickname, the 'Wormhole'. Built using smooth concrete as if it were a liquid material, the structure comprises two parts – one with the library's reading space, café and terrace; the other with toilets, showers and bicycle parking – linked by a flowing arch. With their cave-shaped rooms where curved ceilings, walls and floors merge in unpredictable ways, the architects wanted to create a feeling of weightlessness. 'Architecture, art, humanity and nature meet here, opening up a journey of visitors' imaginations to explore and appreciate the meaning that different beauties bring to their lives,' says MAD's Ma Yansong. Designed to hold up to 10,000 books, the terraced reading area facing the sea can also be used for events. The circular openings recall the holes left by the sea in pebbles and cliffs, and allow great views of Haikou Bay, the sky and the surrounding Century Park.

haikou.gov.cn

57 VAC LIBRARY

Ỷ La, Hà Đông, Hanoi, Vietnam

TO VISIT BEFORE YOU DIE BECAUSE

Growing minds but also plants, the VAC Library by Farming Architects reframes the traditional reading space in an innovative wooden box.

This unique library takes its name from the abbreviation of the Vietnamese phrase 'Vuon-Ao-Chuong', which refers to production systems combining three components: horticulture, aquaculture and animal husbandry. It is part of Farming Architects' attempt to integrate sustainable, high-tech agriculture into urban spaces. 'The core feature is the aquaponics, a system that combines conventional aquaculture [raising aquatic animals] with hydroponics [cultivating plants in water] in a symbiotic environment,' explains its founder An Viet Dung. The cubist wooden frame, where niches between the beams can be customised to hold everything from planters to bookshelves, is an homage to the country's 'do it yourself' attitude. It's also a self-sufficient public space, with solar panels powering both the pump for the aquaponic system and the acrylic cube-shaped lighting that creates a warm ambient feel. Here you will find books but also vegetables, koi carp and chickens – a miniature ecosystem that is also a perfect learning space, climbing frame and peaceful outdoor reading room in a busy city.

farmingarchitects.com

58 THAI BINH LAU ROYAL LIBRARY

Hue Imperial City, Hue, Vietnam

TO VISIT BEFORE YOU DIE BECAUSE

Miraculously intact, this historic reading room sits at the heart of the Hue citadel, the political and cultural heart of Vietnam.

The Royal Library was the only monument left undamaged in the Imperial Citadel after the reoccupation of Hue by French troops in early 1947, and the beautiful building also somehow managed to survive the American bombs of the 1968 Battle of Hue. Known as the Peace Pavilion, it is here that the Nguyen emperors came to read, rest and write poetry. Dating from the 1840s, the two-storey wooden building is elaborately decorated with gloriously colourful mosaics and faces a tranquil pond and rock garden. Fittingly, it sits next to the Pavilion of No Worry and the Morale Improving Room, and was designed as a place of contemplation and betterment as much as a space to store the emperors' precious volumes. The authorities have been slowly but surely restoring Hue's ancient buildings, and just to the north of the UNESCO site you will find another library, the newly reopened Thang Tho Chamber. Built on an island in the middle of a pond to prevent fire but abandoned for over 75 years, the national library founded by the Nguyen dynasty is now home to a research library and small museum.

hue.gov.vn

59 SALT GALATA

Bankalar Caddesi 11, Karaköy, 34421 Istanbul, Turkey

TO VISIT BEFORE YOU DIE BECAUSE

Located in a grand former bank building, this culture and research institution has a wealth of resources – as well as a Michelin-starred restaurant, Neolokal.

Located in the harbourside district of Karaköy, the Salt Galata building was designed by architect Alexandre Vallaury as the headquarters of the Imperial Ottoman Bank. Beautifully restored in 2011, it now houses a specialised library, an auditorium and exhibition spaces designed by Autoban. Focusing primarily on Türkiye, the Eastern Mediterranean and Eastern Europe, Salt Galata's collection contains over 100,000 print resources, mostly on society, geography, art and design. Light bounces off the black-and-white tiles and cream walls of the elegant central atrium, a stunning reading room with curved desks and stylish bookcases. You can go down to the bank's vaults, where there is a small museum showing how the bank notes were stored, or book a slot to use the research library. The ground floor is home to a café and bookshop, while the first floor offers views of the Golden Horn. The cherry on top is Neolokal, where Michelin-starred chef Maksut Aşkar serves fine Turkish wines and carefully presented vegetarian specialities on a fabulous terrace.

saltonline.org +90 212 334 2200

60 JAFFNA PUBLIC LIBRARY

Clock Tower Road, South, Jaffna, Sri Lanka

TO VISIT BEFORE YOU DIE BECAUSE

Jaffna's landmark public library has risen from its ashes to become once again a peaceful temple to learning and reading.

Book burning is sadly not a thing of the past, and biblioclasm has been committed recently by Russian nationalists in Ukraine, Salafi militants in Yemen, ISIS in Mosul and Catholics in Canada. But perhaps the most violent 21st-century example of this deliberate destruction is the burning of the Jaffna library, a symbol of Tamil cultural heritage, in an arson attack in 1981. At the time, it was one of the biggest libraries in Asia, and irreplaceable Tamil manuscripts and palm leaf scrolls went up in flames. Rebuilt, then bombed and turned into a no man's zone during the war, the library rose once again from its ashes in 2001, fully restored and now with added Wi-Fi. Strolling past a statue of Saraswati, the Hindu goddess of learning, in its lush garden today, it's hard to believe that the bright white, dome-capped 1930s building was once left in ruin. On Sunday afternoons, its airy reading room, lit by tall teak-framed windows, is packed with patrons. Visitors are only allowed in the periodical section, and you'll need to take off your shoes before entering.

+94 212 226 028

61 OMAH LIBRARY

Jl. Taman Amarilis 2 F2/15, Taman Villa Meruya, Meruya Utara, Jakarta 11620, Indonesia

TO VISIT BEFORE YOU DIE BECAUSE

Located in an architect's own house, this library aims to foster dialogue on architecture and its many possibilities.

Founded in 2014, On Meeting Architecture Hub (OMAH) stems from architect Realrich Sjarief's desire to continue the discussions started as part of his university course 'How to Think Like an Architect' in a dedicated space. The 1,500-volume-strong, non-profit library and study space, Guha Boboto, is actually based in Sjarief's private home, which he shares with his family. 'Our favourite aspect of this library is how it feels like a cosy home filled with knowledge, making working, learning and reading truly enjoyable,' they say. 'It also offers a quiet space where people can focus, think and at the same time connect with many visitors who always add new stories to this library space.' Here you can explore themes such as stone architecture, brick patterns and everyday materials; learn about traditional architecture and local culture; and network with fellow architecture lovers. Featuring circular windows, glass floors, bamboo details and a leafy courtyard, the space is full of personality. It's also a true cultural hub, with a rich programme of events and classes. The library is accessible by reservation only.

omahlibrary.org

+62 81 6164 4022

62 UMIMIRAI LIBRARY

I-1-1 Jichumachi, Kanazawa, Ishikawa 920-0341, Japan

TO VISIT BEFORE YOU DIE BECAUSE

This three-storey building with a polka dot façade has no ceiling lights – instead it is lit by thousands of little portholes and matching circular desk lights.

Japan has a long tradition of beautiful packaging and exquisitely presented gifts. Here in Kanazawa, the public library comes all wrapped up in a gorgeous 'cake box' perforated façade, courtesy of Kazumi Kudo and Hiroshi Horiba of Japanese firm Coelacanth K&H Architects. The library consists of a large reading room and offices measuring 45m by 45m, with 12m-high ceilings. The entire space is white and filled with a soft, diffuse light thanks to around 6,000 small circular openings in three different sizes. They look like bubbles floating on the sea, but their shape and size is the result of the architects' careful experimenting to optimise the lighting for reading. Thanks to the dappled light and 25 supporting pillars, the main reading room has a slightly otherworldly atmosphere, resembling a minimalist forest where readers can find a spot in a 'clearing' to enjoy one of the thousands of books on offer. There are also workshop and meeting spaces, a hall and a children's library with a read-aloud room and minimalist flower-shaped ceiling lights. Photography is not allowed inside.

lib.kanazawa.ishikawa.jp +81 76 266 2011

63 THIKSEY GOMPA LIBRARY

Thiksey Monastery, Ladakh, Jammu and Kashmir, India

TO VISIT BEFORE YOU DIE BECAUSE

Built in the early 15th century, this 12-storey monastery complex is filled with precious handwritten volumes wrapped in colourful fabrics.

Monastic libraries were key repositories of knowledge in medieval Europe, and the story is no different throughout Asia, where generations of monks have guarded and studied precious scrolls. This is still the case at Thiksey Monastery, near India's border with Tibet. Known as the 'mini Potala of India' due to its resemblance to the Lhasa palace, the monastery is perched on a steep outcrop overlooking the Indus Valley, its white, red and ochre buildings clinging to the hillside. Next to the central shrine in its main prayer hall are several painted and handwritten books as well as 225 volumes of the Tengyur, wrapped in golden silk. The complex's modern library, inaugurated in 2018 by the Dalai Lama, is used by monks but also local students. On the top floor, next to the official residence of the head lama, you might also be able to visit the Lamokhang Temple and library, which is filled with more cloth-bound books and precious scriptures. Above on the rooftop terrace, there are stunning views of the surrounding snowy mountain peaks.

leh.nic.in/tourism

64 MATSUBARA LIBRARY

3 Chome-1-46 Taijo, Matsubara, Osaka 580-0044, Japan

TO VISIT BEFORE YOU DIE BECAUSE

A fortress of a library built in a pond, this is a book-filled, large-scale version of the traditional Japanese rock garden.

When it came to rebuilding the outdated public library in Matsubara, the team at MARU.architecture didn't have to go far for inspiration: they found it in the site's reservoir, which the city had intended to fill in to build the new library. Instead, the architects incorporated it into their design, which appears to be floating on a pond that is not only carpeted with lotus flowers but also helps cool down the new building, opened in 2019. The library's monolithic form, inspired by the city's ancient stone tombs, is also incredibly strong. 'The exterior walls were designed to bear all the horizontal forces of an earthquake; they are made of 600mm-thick pink reinforced concrete, about three times thicker than usual,' write the Tokyo-based architects Yohei Takano and Sachiko Morita. They are pierced by carefully positioned windows that frame the pond and let both light and breeze flow into the reading room and airy walkways. Readers and students love the stylish yet cosy interiors, outdoor seating areas and leafy rooftop terrace.

trc-matsubara.jp +81 72 334 8060

65 DAVID SASSOON LIBRARY

152 Mahatma Gandhi Road, Opp. Jehangir Art Gallery, Kala Ghoda, Fort, Mumbai-400001, India

TO VISIT BEFORE YOU DIE BECAUSE

This recently renovated historic listed building is a fine example of Mumbai's Victorian Gothic architecture and a cultural hub for the city's art district.

Located in the Kala Ghoda art district, the David Sassoon Library dates back to 1847, when a group of young mechanics from the Royal Mint and Government Dockyard formed an association to promote learning and knowledge. A few years later, David Sassoon, a renowned banker and philanthropist, donated ₹60,000 to establish the library. Completed in 1870, its stunning Victorian Gothic structure features arched windows with wooden shutters and a first-floor veranda, on which members can settle with a good book on a planter's chair. Pass the statue of Sassoon in the lobby and you will find patterned Minton tiles and ornate balustrades as well as a leafy courtyard. The main reading room has soaring Burma teak ceilings, banker's lamps and walls lined with glass-enclosed bookcases, home to 30,000 books in five languages. To visit it you will have to either buy an annual membership, or attend one of the special events and book launches held throughout the year. The library is open to the public during the Kala Ghoda Arts Festival and for its annual foundation day celebrations.

davidsassoonlibrary.com

+91 22 2281 5189

66 TIANYI LIBRARY

Tianyi Street, Haishu District, Ningbo, Zhejiang 315010, China

TO VISIT
BEFORE YOU DIE
BECAUSE

China's oldest intact library, this pavilion in a peaceful traditional garden perfectly showcases the ingenuity, beliefs and elaborate designs of the Ming Dynasty.

When the imperial governor and scholar Fan Qin retired in his hometown of Ningbo, a city to the south of Shanghai, he decided to gather the best knowledge of the time to build his ideal library. Constructed in around 1560, the building is influenced by the ancient art of feng shui, while its auspicious name is based on the *I Ching* ancient divination text. The focus here is to guard the library against devastating fires, in any way possible, from the protective high brick walls and alleyways to the adjoining pond and wave decorations on the roof. And this purpose appears even in more esoteric details, such as a layout reflecting the number six, traditionally associated with water. The ground floor is for reading and writing, with a wall of carved wooden shutters that open directly onto the garden, while the darker upper floor is for storing books. They are stacked in bundles inside a series of cupboards, with bags of herbs to repel insects and pieces of gypsum to absorb damp. Apart from fire, the other great enemy of libraries is theft, which is why a set of framed library rules warns Qin's family to let no one ever take a book out of the walled garden complex.

67 CHILDREN'S BOOK FOREST

1 Chome-1-28 Nakanoshima, Kita Ward, Osaka 530-0005, Japan

TO VISIT BEFORE YOU DIE BECAUSE

Pritzker Prize-winning architect Tadao Ando's gift to his hometown is an imaginative riverside library filled with books donated by local supporters.

Osaka is known as 'the people's city' due to the importance of civic engagement. So, of course, its main children's library reflects this community spirit. It is located on a narrow riverside site in the historic centre, the island of Nakanoshima, but feels spacious and airy thanks to the great skills of its Osaka-born architect, Tadao Ando. Aiming to stimulate the curiosity of children as they explore 'the forest of books', it is a labyrinthine space of stairs and bridges, with bookshelves that wrap around curved walls and a three-storey atrium. There are cosy nooks, a cave-like reading space beneath the main staircase and a cylindrical room lit by a central skylight. The books are divided into 12 different themes, including 'Let's Play with Nature', 'Beautiful Things' and 'Eat'. In the boutique, you can buy cute tote bags as well as colouring pencils (but don't use those on the library books!). The library should soon be covered in ivy, and from the terrace overlooking the Dojima River, you can admire a giant green apple sculpture, as well as rows of cherry blossom trees – another Ando initiative.

kodomohonnomori.osaka   +81 66 204 0808

68 SEASHORE LIBRARY

Aranya Gold Coast, Beidaihe New Area, Qinhuangdao, Hebei 316939, China

TO VISIT BEFORE YOU DIE BECAUSE

Also known as 'the Lonely Library', Vector Architects' minimalist concrete building offers space for reading and meditation with views of the East China Sea.

On one of Hebei's long golden beaches, about a three-hour drive east from Beijing, something quite unique has washed up on the seashore. Built as part of an art-and-nature-orientated holiday complex in the trendy seaside resort of Aranya, the Seashore Library is designed to explore the 'shifting light, the breeze flowing through, and the ocean view,' explains its architect, Dong Gong. Completed in 2015, the project celebrates the beauty and texture of the wood grain patterns left by the timber formwork used to build its concrete elements. It houses a main reading area with a wavy ceiling, designed to make the most of the ever-changing ocean views and flooded with natural light, as well as a darker meditation room. The latter is a dramatic space lit by two long and narrow openings that capture the light of sunrise and sunset, and where you can focus on the sound of the ocean rather than the views. The area is home to Vector Architects' Chapel of Music, a beautiful art centre by Neri&Hu, and UCCA Dune Art Museum by Open Architecture. The library is closed during the winter.

aranya.cc

69 RAZA LIBRARY

Hamid Manzil, behind Jama Masjid, Quilla, Rampur, Uttar Pradesh 244901, India

TO VISIT BEFORE YOU DIE BECAUSE

Housed in a magnificent nawab's palace, Raza Library is one of the most significant repositories of Indo-Islamic cultural heritage in India.

Part of Rampur Fort, the palace of Hamid Manzil was built in the early 20th century by Nawab Hamid Ali Khan, who commissioned his chief engineer W.C. Wright to create a suitably grand building for him to hold court. In the 1950s, it was turned into a library for the precious collection of manuscripts and Mughal miniature paintings collected by his forebears. Today the great hall, once home to the nawab's throne and decorated with ornate columns, chandeliers and a gilded ceiling, is a museum showcasing the Raza Library's treasures. They range from astronomical instruments to 17,000 rare manuscripts, 205 handwritten palm leaves, and thousands of printed books in languages including Persian and Sanskrit. The library's collection of paintings includes works by some of India's most famous artists, including Raja Ravi Varma and Abanindranath Tagore. There are also reading rooms for the many researchers who come to pore over the beautiful Arabic calligraphy found in priceless documents such as a 13th-century Koran inlaid in gold and lapis lazuli. The library is free to enter but you will need your passport to go through security.

70 LIBRARY OF CELSUS

Ephesus Archaeological Site, Atatürk,
35920 Selçuk/Izmir, Turkey

TO VISIT BEFORE YOU DIE BECAUSE

The finest surviving example of a Roman library can be found in the ancient capital of Ephesus, on Türkiye's Aegean coast.

Dating from AD 135 and destroyed by a series of earthquakes, the Library of Celsus lay in ruins for centuries until its façade was reconstructed in the 1970s. It was built to commemorate the governor of the Roman province of Asia, Tiberius Julius Celsus Polemaeanus, by his son, whose instructions stipulated that new books – and wreaths for the statues – should be purchased regularly for the library. Unusually, the building includes a crypt, where Celsus was buried in a marble sarcophagus. The façade is decorated with columns and statues representing Sophia (wisdom), Arete (diligence), Ennoia (understanding) and Episteme (erudition) – all virtues still necessary today to make a great librarian. The front windows would have illuminated a large room with three levels of small niches, where 12,000 Greek and Roman papyrus scrolls were stored in wooden cupboards. There are double walls to help control temperature and humidity, as well as a traditional long stone platform running underneath the book niches. It's easy to imagine scholars in togas perched on the plinth, listening to a lecture on Seneca's stoicism or Ptolemy's astronomical discoveries.

muze.gov.tr +90 232 892 6010

COS·TERT·IMP·TRIBVNIC
CAESARIS AVGVSTI
PATRONIS

71 SEOUL CHEONGUN LITERATURE LIBRARY

40 Jahamun-ro 36-gil, Jongno-gu, Seoul, South Korea

TO VISIT BEFORE YOU DIE BECAUSE

Both thoroughly traditional and completely contemporary, this serene library encapsulates South Korea's contrasting architectural styles.

Although it might look like it has been welcoming readers at the foot of Seoul's Inwangsan Mountain for centuries, the Cheongun Literature Library is actually a new building, built in 2014 on the site of a former park management office. The upper part is constructed in the style of a traditional hanok building, all wooden beams and handmade roof tiles, and houses reading and seminar rooms. Hidden underneath is a fully functional contemporary library, its colourful children's section dotted with circular skylights and sunken seating. After they've chosen from 40,000 books downstairs, patrons can head up to the traditional part and read to the sound of birds chirping, or in a pavilion overlooking a waterfall. Around the library is a 3km-long art-themed trail where you can follow in the footsteps of the famous poet Yun Dong-ju and artist Gyeomjae Jeong Seon. And for a truly ancient South Korean library, you'll need to travel to the remote Haeinsa Monastery, since 1398 home to the *Tripitaka Koreana* – all the Buddhist scriptures carved onto 81,350 wooden printing blocks.

jfac.or.kr/site/main/content/chungwoon01 +82 70 4680 4032

청운문학도서관
청운문학도서관

72 STARFIELD LIBRARY

COEX Mall, 513 Yeongdong-daero, Gangnam District,
Seoul 06164, South Korea

TO VISIT
BEFORE YOU DIE
BECAUSE

Now a popular tourist attraction, this shopping mall library shows there are plenty of different ways to bring books and culture to people.

As well as housing food courts and boutiques, malls in Asia are home to the likes of indoor amusement parks, fountain shows and waterways with gondolas, so the idea of placing a giant library at the centre of a huge shopping complex is actually not that far-fetched. At Starfield Library in Seoul's COEX Mall (where there's also an aquarium, by the way), anyone is welcome to take a break and immerse themselves in a good book or magazine. There are 50,000 volumes in various languages to choose from – although the ones on the unreachable top shelves, which stretch for 13m all the way to the glass roof, are decorative only. The 2,800 sq m atrium has a wraparound mezzanine with a café and slightly quieter seating areas, while the events programme includes lectures, concerts and author visits. It's proven so popular with readers (and those who just want to take a selfie on the escalator) that Starfield has opened an equally spectacular library in Suwon, to the south of the capital.

starfield.co.kr/coexmall/main.do +82 2 6002 3031

73 SHANGHAI LIBRARY EAST

300 Hehuan Lu, Pudong, Shanghai 201204, China

TO VISIT BEFORE YOU DIE BECAUSE

Evoking a scholar's rock in a Chinese garden, this beautifully detailed, art-filled cultural hub appears to float above Shanghai's Century Park.

Designed by Schmidt Hammer Lassen (SHL), a Danish studio specialising in stunning libraries from Aarhus (page 15) to Christchurch (page 212), Shanghai Library East is one of the largest new libraries in the world. Opened in 2022, the library 'embraces the idea of collection to connection – a space to bring people together,' writes Chris Hardie of SHL's Shanghai studio. The ultramodern building is actually based on classical traditions: its shape recalls the Taihu stones Chinese scholars used for inspiration and meditation, while its exterior creates a 'cover' of panels etched with photographs of marble swirls. As well as 4.8 million books, it offers a rich programme of lectures and workshops, some held in a central atrium lined with oak and bamboo. There are also play spaces and outdoor reading rooms, and panoramic views of the cityscape throughout. Wonderful site-specific artworks on the theme of text include an abstract, newspaper-inspired terrazzo pattern by Shen Fan in the atrium and a flock of 800 white 'bird' characters by Xu Bing in the main reading room.

74 WATER DROP LIBRARY

Pinghai Town, Huidong, Huizhou City,
Guangdong Province, China

TO VISIT BEFORE YOU DIE BECAUSE

Formed of 'a circle plus a straight line', this library combines views of water, sky and the sea thanks to a unique water feature on its circular roof.

Just east of Hong Kong in China's Guangdong Province is Shuangyue Bay, or 'Double Moon Bay', a holiday destination named after its two crescent-shaped sandy beaches. And hiding among the tower blocks full of holiday-makers is the moon-shaped Water Drop Library, by 3andwich Deisign|He Wei Studio. Built in 2022 to provide a public library for the developing seaside resort, the 450 sq m building is perched on a hill overlooking the South China Sea. Its geometric shape and low profile both respond to the topography and make sure not to block any sea views from nearby residences. A winding path up the hill leads to a straight outdoor corridor sheltered by a long wall, and the pearl-shaped pool, which is actually the roof of the library. The architects refer to it as 'an underwater library', where you can dive into a book in a peaceful environment, sitting by the floor-to-ceiling glass windows of the circular reading room, where bookshelves extend to form a cloud-like shape. Facilities include a private tea room and a bar lit by a skylight placed in the centre of the pool.

thailicloudhuizhou.cn +86 075 2653 7666

75 TAINAN PUBLIC LIBRARY

No. 255 Kangqiao Boulevard, Yongkang District,
Tainan City 710038, Taiwan

TO VISIT BEFORE YOU DIE BECAUSE

Taking their cues from the local culture, expert library architects Mecanoo have designed a state-of-the-art contemporary library for the oldest city in Taiwan.

Inspired by the tiered roofs of the city's 17th-century Confucius Temple, Dutch architects Mecanoo and Taiwanese MAYU have come up with an inverted stepped shape for Tainan's new landmark library, which opened in 2021 in the city's northern Yongkang District. The cantilevered top floor is supported by a series of slender columns, in a modern interpretation of the bamboo forest, and clad with aluminium slats carved with flower patterns that recall the old town's decorative latticed windows. The 37,000 sq m space comes with all the latest technologies, over a million books (including more than 16,000 from the Japanese occupation period), a 24/7 study room, exhibition spaces, and a theatre and conference hall at the top. At the building's core is a double-height wood-clad atrium and sculptural deep-red staircase, with further splashes of colour coming from yellow carpets. Patrons can watch a movie in an alcove in the media library or get some fresh air in one of the library's many sunken patios and roof gardens.

www.tnpl.tn.edu.tw +886 6303 5855

76 NOT JUST LIBRARY

No. 133 Guangfu South Road, Xinyi District, Taipei City, Taiwan 110

TO VISIT BEFORE YOU DIE BECAUSE

The clue is in the name: this cultural space, opened in 2020 in a former bathhouse, is about more than books – it's a whole immersive experience.

Nearly a century ago, this bathhouse welcomed the female workers of the Songshan tobacco factory after a long day at work. Commissioned by the Taiwan Design Research Institute, JC. Architecture & Design have decided to celebrate the utilitarian space's original features, preserving everything from the patterned tiles to the wooden windows. The tiled floors have been repaired with gold fillings, in the spirit of kintsugi, while the scent of books has replaced that of soap. The Book Bath features sunken seating and over 10,000 books and magazines on lifestyle, design and architecture on birch plywood bookshelves. Here, patrons can 'enjoy being bathed in spirits and knowledge, immersing themselves in invisible thoughts,' writes Johnny Chiu, the founder of JC. Architecture & Design. The second reading area is a semicircular tiled space with the old bath, and a desk stretching along the wall. The space hosts concerts and lectures with some events also taking place in the wonderful patio garden, filled with greenery and illuminated by floor lamps. Also in Taipei is the Beitou Public Library, Taiwan's first environmentally friendly library. Designed by Kuo Ying-chao, it is located next to the Beitou Hot Spring Museum.

tdri.org.tw +886 2 2745 8199

77 TIANJIN BINHAI LIBRARY

Fudong Middle Road, Binhai County, Yancheng, Jiangsu 224500, China

TO VISIT BEFORE YOU DIE BECAUSE

At the centre of MVRDV's library is an otherworldly giant eye that watches you through a glass façade lined with flowing bookshelves.

Unless you live in China, it's unlikely you'll have heard of Tianjin, a megalopolis of over 13 million inhabitants on the Bohai Sea. But this – literally eye-catching – 2007 library has certainly put it on the map. While Tianjin's historic heart lies inland along the Hai River, its futuristic new soul lies in coastal Binhai, where a whole new cultural district has sprung up. Innovative Dutch studio MVRDV has turned what could have been just a boring glass box (masterplanners GMP had stipulated a large rectangular building) into a spectacular five-level library lined with flowing, cascading bookshelves that encircle a central 'folly', a spherical auditorium. 'The Eye hollows out the building and creates, out of bookshelves, an environment to sit, to read, to hang out, to climb and to access, to create an organic social space,' writes MVRDV co-founder Winy Maas. The architects had planned access for all the bookshelves, but this idea was abandoned by the client, which means the top shelves are lined with aluminium plates printed with books rather than real volumes.

bhwhzx.cn/library.aspx   +86 22 6554 5678

78 TAMA ART UNIVERSITY LIBRARY

2 Chome-1723 Yarimizu, Hachioji, Tokyo 192-0394, Japan

TO VISIT BEFORE YOU DIE BECAUSE

An abstract landscape with soaring concrete arches and a sloping floor, this library is a masterpiece by Pritzker Architecture Prize laureate Toyo Ito.

Tama Art University is one of Japan's leading art and design universities, so it's no wonder its Hachioji Library boasts a unique concept by Toyo Ito. 'Since all buildings on the campus are made of exposed concrete, our design is also of exposed concrete. But the architectural vocabulary of this building is completely different from the others,' writes the award-winning architect. Completed in 2007, the structure is composed of intersecting, 20cm-thick arches with different spans that appear to be flying above the campus gardens. Although slender, they are very strong, thanks to hidden steel elements and a seismic isolation structure. 'A light and rhythmic space is achieved by placing arches with tapered footings continuously in different directions; but the interior space as a whole has a sense of tranquillity and transparency,' says Ito. Another surprising element is the sloping ground floor, constructed to match the site's slope and create a closer relationship with the surroundings.

tamabi.ac.jp/english/about/library +81 42 676 8611

79 LIBRARY IN RUINS

Sunyao, Xiuwu, Jiaozuo, Henan 454361, China

TO VISIT BEFORE YOU DIE BECAUSE

This clever, tiny library in an old mountain village is part of a network of cultural pavilions that aim to bring culture and fun to a large rural area.

When architect Chen Xi of Shenzhen-based Atelier Xi was commissioned by the county of Xiuwu, in the province of Henan in central China, to build a library for the rural community, his brief included a big and shiny 300 sq m building. What they got instead is rather different: a series of cast-in-place concrete miniature public spaces, scattered around villages and with unique designs. The concept is perfectly adapted to the library's vast serving area, spread over 630 sq km and with few transport links. They include a pink pavilion overlooking a sea of peach trees, a floating theatre, a geometric library in a chrysanthemum field and this 66 sq m Library in Ruins, located in the village of Sunyao. Opened in 2020, it grows out of the remnants of an abandoned adobe house, with traditional wooden doors and an undulating first floor. Inside there is a stepped reading area/projection room, while the rooftop has more seating and a slide, as well as views of the old village and surrounding mountains. The small plaza in front of the building regularly hosts community activities and festivals.

80 YUSUHARA COMMUNITY LIBRARY

1212-2 Yusuhara, Takaoka District, Kochi 785-0610, Japan

TO VISIT BEFORE YOU DIE BECAUSE

The perfect home for book lovers, this Kengo Kuma-designed library has lots of unique touches, including a grand piano and a bouldering wall.

Despite its striking architecture, this community library in Yusuhara in the Shikoku Mountains (known as the 'town above the clouds') is a homely space, popular with locals young and old. Swap your shoes for slippers before exploring the building, one of six designed for the community by renowned architect Kengo Kuma using locally sourced cedar wood. The wooden flooring gives the reading room a warm and welcoming feeling, while the ceiling's forest of beams recalls the traditional structure of the nearby covered wooden bridge. It adds a dynamic background to the space, which has a raised area that can be used as a stage for events. There's also a grand piano, a cosy children's section, a lounge where you can read art books and manga on comfy sofas and even a bouldering wall. There's often music in the background, and activities like chair yoga and film screenings. Plus, you can enjoy a cheesecake in the café, run by a support group for people with disabilities.

kumonoue-lib.jp

+81 88 965 1900

YURURI ゆすはら
yururi yusuhara

81 WILLIAM W. COOK LEGAL RESEARCH LIBRARY

801 Monroe Street, Ann Arbor, Michigan 48109, USA

TO VISIT BEFORE YOU DIE BECAUSE

One of the largest academic law libraries in the world, it is housed in a series of stunning buildings ranging from Collegiate Gothic to International Style.

It seems that about a century ago, every single university in North America was craving its own Gothic Revival campus. From Yale to Harvard, the Collegiate Gothic style was born, and here in Ann Arbor, Michigan, there is a stunning example of the genre, in the shape of this research library, part of the University of Michigan Law School. Home to over a million volumes and nearly as many gargoyles and turrets, it was built in the 1930s and is known for its cathedral-like main reading room, said to be inspired by King's College Chapel in Cambridge, England. 'An amazing feature of the library is the view of the original building from the Underground Library,' says Kincaid C. Brown, director of the University of Michigan Law Library. 'The view of the reading room's façade through the Underground's massive skylights is a breathtaking juxtaposition.' Both are open to the public, so you can admire for yourself the contrast between Gunnar Birkerts' 1980s clean-lined International Style addition and the reading room's stained-glass windows and heavy chandeliers.

michigan.law.umich.edu

82 AUSTIN CENTRAL LIBRARY

710 W César Chávez Street, Austin, Texas 78701, USA

TO VISIT BEFORE YOU DIE BECAUSE

Flooded with natural light, this eco-friendly landmark has become a vibrant community hub packed with colourful details and welcoming nooks.

From humble beginnings in the 1920s, in a rented room filled with donated books, to this high-tech glass building complete with roof garden: the Austin Central Library has always evolved with the times, and its latest iteration is designed to be flexible enough to serve the community for the next hundred years. Located in the Seaholm EcoDistrict, the flagship library opened in 2017 on the site of a former power plant, overlooking Shoal Creek and Lady Bird Lake. It was designed in collaboration with Lake Flato Architects and Shepley Bulfinch and aspires to be the most day-lit public library, thanks to its six-storey atrium. 'The unique rooftop butterfly garden and reading porches, inspired by Texans' love for the outdoors, draw visitors to connect with nature,' write the architects of their LEED Platinum-certified green building. It is also home to makerspaces, a bookshop, a café and an event centre, as well as an art gallery featuring rotating art displays from local and national artists.

library.austintexas.gov

+1 512 974 7400

83 GEORGE PEABODY LIBRARY

17 E Mt Vernon Place, Baltimore, Maryland 21202, USA

TO VISIT BEFORE YOU DIE BECAUSE

Widely regarded as one of the most beautiful libraries in the world, this soaring 'Cathedral of Books' is the finest surviving example of an iron-stack library.

The mid-19th century saw the opening of scores of new public libraries financed by rich philanthropists, and perhaps the most spectacular of them all is this reading room in Baltimore, funded by self-made businessman George Peabody. Before his death, he donated his fortune to charitable causes, including the foundation of the Peabody Institute in the city where he had started out as a trader, in appreciation of the citizens' 'kindness and hospitality'. Now part of the Johns Hopkins University, the institute's library was designed in 1878 by local architect Edmund Lind, and features an impressive neo-Greco central atrium lined with five tiers of ornamental iron bookcases. Steam-driven dumbwaiters and a pneumatic tube system once helped librarians fetch books from the upper floors, which rise up to a central skylight, 18m above a black-and-white marble floor. The library's collection of nearly 300,000 volumes, mainly from the 19th century, is neatly organised in a card catalogue and includes first editions by Edgar Allan Poe and Darwin.

library.jhu.edu +1 667 208 6715

84 VIRGILIO BARCO LIBRARY

Av. La Esmeralda #57–60, Teusaquillo, Bogotá, Colombia

TO VISIT BEFORE YOU DIE BECAUSE

A Bogotá landmark, this circular brick library offers a series of tranquil reading rooms and outdoor spaces opening out onto water features and greenery.

The late, great Colombian architect Rogelio Salmona was renowned for his mastery of the humble red brick, and for using natural shapes such as spirals and curves in his projects. His 2001 design for a new public library in Bogotá perfectly encapsulates his approach, which builds on his experience as a draftsman for Le Corbusier. Part of the Simón Bolívar Metropolitan Park, the swirling library is built slightly below ground level, encircled by a moat-like reflective pool and grassy slopes. These, along with the building's pedestrian walkways and courtyards, help to make the surrounding cityscape disappear, creating a calm and peaceful atmosphere. It looks a bit like the patterned shell of a snail from above and is equally intricate from the inside, which comprises, among other things, a collection of 150,000 volumes, reference and speciality rooms and an auditorium (there's also an outdoor reading area and an open-air theatre). All the furniture, including the bookshelves, was designed by Salmona himself.

biblored.gov.co/bibliotecas/biblioteca-virgilio

+57 601 580 3010

85 SPRINGDALE LIBRARY

10705 Bramalea Road, Brampton, Ontario L6R 0C1, Canada

TO VISIT BEFORE YOU DIE BECAUSE

This highly sustainable, highly unusual library was designed as a gathering space, its open plan fostering a feeling of community.

Completed in 2019 in Brampton, a fast-growing, multicultural suburb of Toronto, this light and airy triangular building is located on a site hemmed in on two sides by a natural ravine. Its architects, RDHA, have added to the topography by creating an undulating green roof that rises and sinks above the reading rooms. An organic skylight dips into the children's library, while a wide dome soars above the main foyer. The layered façades are particularly striking, with curved glass panels, a ceramic pattern, and a screen of stainless steel tubes that vary in density depending on solar orientation. The combination of these vertical elements aims to echo 'the trunks of trees in a forest, and the turning pages of a library book', write the architects. The creative hub is home to a 3D printer, music studio, sticker station and button-making machine, while its reading rooms open onto a courtyard garden, or the greenery of Komagata Maru Park and playground. According to its patrons, it's the perfect place to meet up, relax and read.

bramptonlibrary.ca

+1 905 793 4636

86 CALGARY CENTRAL LIBRARY

800 3 Street SE, Calgary, Alberta T2G 2E7, Canada

TO VISIT BEFORE YOU DIE BECAUSE

It's the award-winning main branch of one of the most actively used library systems in North America, created for and inspired by its diverse inhabitants.

Located on a once-inaccessible site divided by rail tracks, this 22,000 sq m library links Calgary's downtown and East Village, its entry plaza doubling up as a portal and a bridge. This is why its architects, Snøhetta and DIALOG, describe it as a library that 'reconnects a city and its people'. Calgary's most ambitious cultural project since the 1988 Olympic Games, it's also a feat of engineering, constructed above a working train line, and delivered on schedule and within budget in 2018. The façade's hexagonal panels reflect the city and sky, while its curved form is inspired by the ancient oil lamps used for reading. The region's common chinook arch cloud formation is mirrored in The Archway, a pedestrian link framed in local redwood cedar. As well as a performance hall and recording studios, the LEED Gold building houses an Indigenous Languages Resource Centre and a Children's Lodge offering meetings with Elders to explore topics relating to culture, history and reconciliation. There are free daily architectural tours.

calgarylibrary.ca +1 403 260 2600

87 HAROLD WASHINGTON LIBRARY

400 S State Street Chicago, Illinois 60605, USA

TO VISIT BEFORE YOU DIE BECAUSE

The largest public library in the world when it opened in 1991, this proudly different building has found its place in America's first city of architecture.

A 1980s competition for a new central library in Chicago, funded by the Pritzker family, pitted two very different styles against each other: a glass design by Helmut Jahn and a postmodern project by Hammond, Beeby and Babka. The first was deemed too expensive, so the chosen design reflects Hammond and co's penchant for architectural flourishes. Inspired by the nearby Rookery, Auditorium and Monadnock buildings, it features granite blocks and red brick walls, with huge arched windows and details representing the natural bounty of the Midwest. Topped with a magnificent metal and glass roof decorated with large owl figures, it houses makerspaces, an auditorium clad in African cherry wood and the gorgeous Winter Garden. Pick one of the 200,000 novels on offer and sit under its glass dome surrounded by olive trees. Happily, Jahn did get to design his own library in the end: the high-tech, glass-domed 2011 Joe and Rika Mansueto Library at the University of Chicago.

chipublib.org +1 312 747 4300

88 CARNEGIE WEST BRANCH

1900 Fulton Road, Cleveland, Ohio 44113, USA

TO VISIT BEFORE YOU DIE BECAUSE

A triangular building on a triangular site, this fine example of a Carnegie library is a much-loved, buzzing cultural hub dedicated to its multicultural audience.

The Scottish-American philanthropist Andrew Carnegie, also known as the 'Steel King' or 'the good Saint Andrew', funded the construction of over 2,500 libraries worldwide between 1883 and 1929. Between 1903 and 1914, he pledged the equivalent of $20 million to build 15 new libraries in the rapidly growing industrial city of Cleveland. One of these was the Carnegie West Branch, which opened in 1910 after much delay, and only thanks to additional donations from Carnegie – a sign of how much he valued the project and its pioneering librarian, William H. Brett. Experts said the new library 'stood without a peer anywhere in the United States', and it's still easy to see why today. Architect Edward L. Tilton designed a classical façade of contrasting red brick, Berea sandstone and terracotta fluted columns, and interiors decorated with replicas of the Parthenon frieze. It's the beating heart of the community, with an outdoor Storywalk, a children's room complete with a farm truck, a programme of fun events throughout the year and a long tradition of welcoming all readers, whatever their native language.

cpl.org/location/carnegiewest +1 216 623 6927

FRIENDS

89 DONALD DUNGAN LIBRARY

1855 Park Avenue, Costa Mesa, California 92627, USA

TO VISIT BEFORE YOU DIE BECAUSE

Inspired in part by Eero Saarinen's TWA Flight Center, this dynamic library stands out for its custom-designed skylights and soaring white curves.

The curvy white, alabaster concrete-plastered façade of this Orange County library pays homage to Southern California's adobe Mission-style architecture, but also to the sleek, mid-century lines of the region's key aerospace industry. Built by Los Angeles-based architects Johnson Favaro as part of a masterplan to redevelop an urban park, the two-storey library features dramatic curves, recessed cut-outs and large arched windows, carefully placed to both harness natural light and minimise direct sun exposure. Recalling high-end hotel lounges, the interiors by RVD Associates and Diane Lam Design are particularly plush, with porcelain tile flooring and rich white oak shelving. Sit on a Patricia Urquiola chair in the light-filled upstairs reading room and admire the surrounding green space. Replacing a car park, it has shaded reading areas and space for community events. If you're in the area, we also recommend taking a peek at the nearby Huntington Beach Central Library, a Richard Neutra-designed brutalist building complete with indoor gardens and concrete terraces.

ocpl.org/libraries/costa-mesa-donald-dungan

+1 949 646 8845

90 DENVER CENTRAL LIBRARY

10 W 14th Avenue Parkway, Denver, Colorado 80204, USA

TO VISIT BEFORE YOU DIE BECAUSE

One of the country's largest libraries, this truly unique building comes with Edward Ruscha murals, and fossils embedded in the floor of its main hall.

Located in Downtown Denver's Golden Triangle, this giant library stands its ground in an area known for its eye-catching buildings, not least its neighbours at the Denver Art Museum, designed by Gio Ponti and Daniel Libeskind. It first opened in the 1950s, replacing the Carnegie-built libraries it had outgrown with a modern design by Burnham F. Hoyt. This listed building is still in use but forms only a small part of the new library, completely remodelled in 1995 by Michael Graves. Finished in limestone in soft south-western colours of buff, red and green, with interiors in maple wood, the building reflects the leading postmodern architect's belief that cultural organisations are the heart of their communities. Executive director Michelle Jeske agrees: 'The library brings together a diverse community and perspectives, upholding a pillar of democracy: public spaces and social capital. In addition to being a trusted source of information, it's a place where anyone can connect with others, learn, explore and thrive.' Highlights of the collection include ancient Babylon clay tablets and one of the largest genealogy collections in the United States.

denverlibrary.org +1 720 865 1111

91 STATE LAW LIBRARY

1007 E Grand Avenue, Des Moines, Iowa 50319, USA

TO VISIT BEFORE YOU DIE BECAUSE

Full of pattern and colour, and filled to the rafters with legal titles, this Victorian research library has to be seen to be believed.

Iowa's five-domed State Capitol is impressive enough from the outside, but its interiors are positively lavish, with grand staircases and lofty corridors clad in 29 different types of marble. On the second floor you will find the equally dazzling State Law Library, where readers can study some of the 100,000 titles after having sifted through the library's original card catalogue (or perhaps just having used the free Wi-Fi...). The dry subject matter stands in complete contrast to the extravagant décor: the breathtaking Victorian-style room features colourful stained-glass windows and encaustic tile floors, while wrought-iron spiral staircases lead to bookcases stretching five storeys high. It's a fittingly impressive space for a state once known for its legal might – Iowa has spearheaded many civil rights, including early adoption or support of Black suffrage, women's rights and same-sex marriage. Like the Capitol building itself, it was designed by French-born architect Alfred Henry Piquenard, and completed by his student William F. Hackney in 1886.

statelibraryofiowa.gov

+1 800 248 4483

92 DETROIT MAIN LIBRARY

5201 Woodward Avenue, Detroit, Michigan 48202, USA

TO VISIT BEFORE YOU DIE BECAUSE

This is the mural-filled star of Detroit's 'City Beautiful' remodelling, which aimed to add beauty, grandeur and civic pride to the fast-growing Motor City.

This is the tale of two architects, a father and son who each had their own take on what would make the ideal public library. The first, Cass Gilbert, built it in white Vermont marble in the Early Italian Renaissance style in 1921, while the second, Cass Gilbert Jr (with Francis Keally), added two modern, clean-lined wings in the 1960s. They are two faces of the same coin, each with their own unique details. Running throughout the spaces is a series of stunning murals by local artists, from Edwin H. Blashfield's allegories to John S. Coppin's transport-themed triptych. Readers' favourites include the former children's library's fireplace, adorned with local Pewabic tiles depicting fairy tales, and Millard Sheets' bright mosaics. The library holds treasures such as George Washington's diary and original manuscripts by Mark Twain and Laura Ingalls Wilder, while special collections celebrate automotive and sporting history. Here you can delve into the role of African Americans in the performing arts, or simply pop in to borrow sheet music, vinyl records, video games or cookbooks.

detroitpubliclibrary.org

+1 313 481 1400

93 DRUMMONDVILLE PUBLIC LIBRARY

425 Rue des Forges, Drummondville, Quebec J2B 0G4, Canada

TO VISIT BEFORE YOU DIE BECAUSE

An innovative pairing of sport and culture, this award-winning, immensely popular library is proudly of its time and of its place.

Curling up with a book inside, or completing a few laps on a freshly resurfaced ice rink – these are the kind of activities that make the long Canadian winters bearable. Both are combined here at Drummondville library, a project that was awarded the Governor General's Medal in Architecture in 2020. Designed by Chevalier Morales with DMA Architectes, the library's rounded corners and translucent façade are inspired by the neighbouring outdoor ice rink (the town boasts the largest number of rinks per inhabitant in the province). They are connected by an energy loop to optimise energy costs for both spaces. Meanwhile, the town's steel and hydropower heritage informed the building's colour (from the pale-blue slag glass left over from steel production) and curves (from the blades of the turbines). Easily accessible by public transport, the new community hub has plenty of books but also towers of CDs and DVDs and a cute courtyard garden. As for the second-floor seating area, it's a great spot from which to view the hockey games in winter.

tourismedrummondville.com

+1 819 478 6573

94 CLASS OF 1945 LIBRARY

Phillips Exeter Academy, 20 Main Street, Exeter,
New Hampshire 03833-2460, USA

TO VISIT
BEFORE YOU DIE
BECAUSE

The world's largest secondary-school library, this awesome brick-and-concrete monument is Louis Kahn's masterpiece.

'A man with a book goes to the light. A library begins that way. He will not go 50 feet away to an electric light,' once explained the great modernist architect Louis Kahn. His design for the Class of 1945 Library, located at the heart of the Phillips Exeter Academy, follows this through. It is suffused with light, with a great central atrium ringed by white oak bookcases, themselves encircled by 210 study carrels placed just next to the windows. The 1971 design completely fulfils the brief of Academy librarian Rodney Armstrong, who said: 'The emphasis should not be on housing books, but on housing readers using books.' Kahn used simple materials such as brick and concrete in new ways to create buildings full of personality, and here at Exeter he was gifted with local Eno water-struck bricks, which the Academy bulk-bought when the company went out of business. To create his masterpiece, Kahn paired over 720,000 of them with travertine, teak panels and the atrium's striking poured concrete geometric elements. The library offers Visitor Days throughout the year.

exeter.edu/library/visiting-the-class-of-1945-library

95 YUYARINA PACHA LIBRARY

Huaticocha, E20, Loreto, Ecuador

TO VISIT BEFORE YOU DIE BECAUSE

A space for knowledge, this rainforest library is a symbol of the ability of rural communities to take charge of their own development and learning.

Located about 100km south-east of Quito, this children's library rises up like a tree house in a clearing of the Amazon rainforest and has its roots in a reading club organised by local associations Laboratorio Creativo Sarawarmi and Witoca. Designed by Quito-based practice Al Borde and completed in 2024, the library and community room is a safe space where children can learn, play and create. It is named Yuyarina Pacha, which means 'space-time to think' in Kichwa. The open ground floor is dedicated to messy art and science workshops; the first floor is home to the book collection, presented on wooden shelves; and the top floor focuses on digital learning and the storage of an audio collection preserving the community's oral memory. Up there is also a balcony reading table, where you can read magazines with your feet dangling in the central void. Embracing the region's ancestral techniques, the structure is made of chonta, an Amazonian palm known for its incredible durability and strength, topped with a steep thatched roof and a glass skylight.

@sarawarmi @witoca_coffee

96 PLAZA BIBLIOTECA SUR

Av. Ricardo Elías Aparicio 740, La Molina, Lima, Peru

TO VISIT BEFORE YOU DIE BECAUSE

Inspired by a row of books lined up on a shelf, this inviting building proves that getting the community on board is key to a successful new library.

There is no better sight for an avid reader than a shelf full of books, and it is this heavenly vision that has inspired the concrete pillars and pink plinth of this library built in 2017 on the outskirts of Lima. A couple of tilting spines mark the main entrance of the building, which was designed by Gonzalez Moix Arquitectura. The 1,300 sq m structure involved eight years of planning and ongoing consultation with the community. Readers can now sit on stone benches on a plaza backdropped by a wood-clad wall, daydream under a tree in the adjoining park or head inside to study among a forest of V-shaped columns. 'It was vital for us to think about the action of sitting to read a book as our starting point and transitioning the exterior landscape towards the interior, and vice versa,' explain the architects. There are around 4,200 books to peruse, as well as an auditorium, a children's library and a Quechua cultural space. Popular workshops ranging from embroidery to computing make the place a bustling hub all week long.

portal.munimolina.gob.pe/plaza-biblioteca-sur

+51 1 754 4000

97 LOS ANGELES CENTRAL LIBRARY

630 W 5th Street, Los Angeles, California 90071, USA

TO VISIT BEFORE YOU DIE BECAUSE

Full of symbolism and ancient Egyptian influences, this early example of art deco is now complemented by a huge extension home to 143km of bookshelves.

Regarded as one of the most innovative projects of New York architect Bertram Goodhue, the Richard J. Riordan Central Library was built in 1926 in LA's historic downtown. Its simple geometric volumes, including a golden pyramid topped with a hand holding the torch of knowledge, are decorated with inscriptions, friezes and sculptures by Lee Lawrie based on the theme of 'Light of Learning'. Inside are colourful stencilled ceilings, black marble sphinxes and bronze chandeliers. You can still see original interiors and murals in the children's department (once the Reference Room), but most books are now stored in the 1990s Tom Bradley Wing, an extension with a large glass atrium. Treasures of the library include over 3 million historic photographs, a vast science and patents department, books in many of the multicultural city's languages and a 100,000-strong collection of ancient maps. Free tours of the building and its art are given every day the library is open, and on Saturdays there is a tour of the beautiful Maguire Gardens surrounding the library.

lapl.org/branches/central-library +1 213 228 7000

98 SANTO DOMINGO SAVIO LIBRARY PARK

Cl. 107a #Cra 33B # 107A-100, Santo Domingo Savio I, Medellín, Colombia

TO VISIT BEFORE YOU DIE BECAUSE

Reachable by cable car, this award-winning rock-shaped cultural complex was designed as part of the transformation of a no-go area.

'Libraries should resemble public spaces more than conventional buildings,' says Giancarlo Mazzanti, the architect of Medellín's Santo Domingo Savio Library Park, which is why this 2007 project (initially known as Biblioteca de España) is spread across three boulder-shaped buildings, clad in dark stone tiles and linked by a leafy public square. As well as a library, they also include a cinema, exercise areas, a preschool and exhibition halls. Slightly fortress-like, with small windows, the project was designed as a place of refuge from the surrounding neighbourhood, once considered one of the most dangerous places in Latin America. In fact, the library became a symbol first of the city's concerted efforts to transform itself, thanks to a network of cable cars, green corridors and new facilities, and later of the difficulties faced by unconventional buildings. Like the best of books, it's had quite a few plot twists – due to serious problems with the façade, it is currently surrounded by scaffolding. Let's hope for a happy ending, and that it can reopen soon and retake its place as a proud city landmark.

99 UNAM CENTRAL LIBRARY

Escolar S/N, Ciudad Universitaria, Alcaldía, Coyoacán, 04510 Mexico City, Mexico

TO VISIT BEFORE YOU DIE BECAUSE

Poetry in mosaics rather than words wraps around this functionalist university library, a UNESCO World Heritage site that is an ode to Mexican culture.

They say don't judge a book by its cover, but sometimes this is exactly the right thing to do... Especially in the case of the 1956 Biblioteca Central at Mexico City's National Autonomous University of Mexico (UNAM). Completely covered in a dizzying array of colourful mosaics, it is the work of Coyoacán-born artist Juan O'Gorman, who studied architecture at UNAM before helping build its landmark library along with Gustavo Saavedra and Juan Martínez de Velasco. 'I spent two days and nights, almost without sleeping or eating, making the first sketches of this enormous mosaic that would cover the four sides of the building's collection tower,' wrote O'Gorman. He visited quarries all around the country to find the most vibrant stones – much more long-lasting than paint – for his artwork, trekking across the Zacatecas desert to find blue chalcedony (he ended up using blue glass). The mosaics illustrate events from Mexico's history and mythology, including Tlaloc, the water god; an Indigenous couple in their traditional clothing; and the revolutionary leader Emiliano Zapata.

 bibliotecacentral.unam.mx +52 55 5622 1625

100 VASCONCELOS LIBRARY

Eje 1 Nte. S/N, Buenavista, Cuauhtémoc, 06350 Mexico City, Mexico

TO VISIT BEFORE YOU DIE BECAUSE

Described by its architects as an 'ark, a carrier of human knowledge, immersed in a lush botanic garden', this urban oasis boasts a vertiginous main hall.

Dedicated to the controversial philosopher José Vasconcelos, this equally thought-provoking library is either a masterpiece of architecture or the ultimate white elephant, depending on who you talk to. Yet locals are fans of this peaceful sanctuary in the heart of the noisy city, which is surrounded by greenery and spreads across a cavernous 210m-long hall. Its Mexican architect Alberto Kalach has turned the idea of a bookshelf upside down – instead of being placed on solid, reinforced floors, here the metal shelves are hung directly from the roof, supported by a network of steel beams and rods. Thin wire balustrades, suspended staircases and glass walkways make the experience of reaching for a book feel slightly more adventurous than elsewhere (we hope the books about vertigo are stored on the ground floor). This exposed skeleton is paired with a whale installation by Gabriel Orozco and filled with over 600,000 volumes. There are also plans to open a café and allow access to the greenhouse, which is not currently open to the public.

 bibliotecavasconcelos.gob.mx

missoula public library

101 MISSOULA PUBLIC LIBRARY

455 E Main Street, Missoula, Montana 59802, USA

TO VISIT BEFORE YOU DIE BECAUSE

This multi-award-winning library combines sustainable architecture, great design, ancient wisdom and an innovative, holistic approach.

Voted IFLA Public Library of the Year in 2022, this vibrant cultural hub serves more than 120,000 residents, most of whom live in small mountain and rural towns. Built following green principles and filled with Indigenous artworks, it's about way more than just free access to books. It 'serves the whole person, engaging all senses' thanks to active play areas, studios, a demonstration kitchen and a Library of Things, and has room for four non-profit community organisations, which help provide workshops and hands-on learning experiences. Completed by MSR Design and A&E Design in 2021, the building is inspired by Montana's idyllic landscapes and geology. Its exterior cladding reflects the dynamic valley weather, while inside, the main staircase is inspired by a popular nearby mountain trail, visible from some of the library's windows. There are cosy cave-like forms, and splashes of bright pink on the children's level – a reference to bitterroot, Montana's state flower.

 missoulapubliclibrary.org +1 406 721 2665

102 THE NATIONAL ARCHIVES IN MONTRÉAL

535 Avenue Viger E, Montréal, Québec H2L 2P3, Canada

TO VISIT BEFORE YOU DIE BECAUSE

Located near Montréal's harbour, this hidden gem of a research library is a haven for those in search of peace and quiet.

Built in 1910 for the HEC Montréal business school and a ten-minute walk from the city's Grande Bibliothèque, the building of the National Archives in Montréal features Mercury, god of commerce, and Minerva, goddess of trade, perched at the top of its grand Beaux Arts façade. Yet inside, it is dedicated not to making money but to celebrating the past: home to part of Québec's national archives, it is a treasure trove for genealogists and historians, who can sift through 15,000 reference works, 100 periodical titles and a collection of 20,000 microfilms. Four giant sculptures of Greek caryatids watch over the passageway leading to the star of the show, the 'salle de consultation', which welcomes up to 200 researchers. It's a bright space with lots of white elements, including a spiral staircase and three levels of galleries with swirling wrought-iron balustrades and translucent glass floors. You'll need your ID to visit.

banq.qc.ca

+1 514 873 1100

103 BEINECKE RARE BOOK & MANUSCRIPT LIBRARY

121 Wall Street, New Haven, Connecticut 06511, USA

TO VISIT BEFORE YOU DIE BECAUSE

This iconic International Style research library holds one of the world's largest collections of rare books and manuscripts.

Standing like a glowing treasure chest on Yale University's Hewitt Quadrangle, the Beinecke Library's marble and granite block hides a six-storey, glass-enclosed tower of books, holding around 180,000 volumes (there's a million more in the basement). Completed in 1963, this box-within-a-box design is the creation of Gordon Bunshaft of Skidmore, Owings & Merrill, and its genius lies in the grid of translucent Vermont marble panels that act as windows and protect the precious collection from direct sunlight. From the outside, all is pale and bright, but from the inside, the sun reveals the marble's veins and creates a warm, honey-coloured space with dark walls and fixtures. Around the glass stack tower are temporary exhibitions, on topics such as the art of protest, and permanent displays including a Gutenberg Bible. The library continues to add to its collections, for example recently acquiring prints by photographer Gordon Parks. Design fans will want to check out the Florence Knoll and Marcel Breuer furniture, as well as the Isamu Noguchi sculpture garden.

beinecke.library.yale.edu

+1 203 432 2977

104 MORGAN LIBRARY & MUSEUM

225 Madison Avenue, New York, New York 10016, USA

TO VISIT BEFORE YOU DIE BECAUSE

Hiding behind a simple pink marble portico, this spectacular library has been opened to the public since 1924, following the wishes of its founder JP Morgan.

Covering half a city block, the Morgan Library & Museum is a mix of various buildings and styles, its most recent addition being a glass entrance by Renzo Piano. But it all started from Mr Morgan's Library, which was built in 1906 for the influential banker near his New York home. It was a much-needed space to store his immense collection of rare books, prints and illuminated manuscripts. Some of them – including a Gutenberg Bible – are still on display today in the flamboyant library designed by Charles F. McKim in the American Renaissance style. Lining its 9m walls are triple-tiers of bronze and walnut bookcases, with balconies accessed via a pair of concealed staircases. Decorations include a 16th-century tapestry warning of the sin of avarice, zodiacal signs, and paintings representing the muses and figures including Dante, Botticelli and Herodotus. Next door is the rotunda, with a stucco ceiling fit for an Italian palazzo; Morgan's majestic study, lit by stained-glass windows; and the former office of librarian Belle da Costa Greene, now a gallery.

themorgan.org

+1 212 685 0008

105 NEW YORK PUBLIC LIBRARY MAIN BRANCH

476 5th Avenue, New York, New York 10018, USA

TO VISIT BEFORE YOU DIE BECAUSE

Located on the site of a former reservoir, this landmark library is a font of knowledge wrapped in a stunning stone building guarded by a pair of famous lions.

The imposing classical marble building of the New York Library that you see on 5th Avenue is only the tip of the iceberg. Below the main reading room are seven floors of steel-framed underground stacks, which once delivered books directly to the reading room above using electric lifts and conveyers. This revolutionary layout by leading librarian Dr John Billings was matched by an elegant Beaux Arts stone by Carrère and Hastings. Now known as the Stephen A. Schwarzman Building, the high-tech library took nine years to construct, finally opening in 1911 – it took a whole year to transfer the books from the former Astor and Lenox Libraries to the new 121km worth of shelves. Its main reading room boasts a 15m-high and 120m-long ceiling, and seats 624 readers. Join a tour to find out more, or admire some of the most extraordinary items of the library's 58-million-strong collection, on display in the Polonsky Exhibition. Treasures on view in the rotating exhibition have included a copy of the 1776 Declaration of Independence, early opera recordings on wax cylinders and original illustrations of *The Wonderful Wizard of Oz*.

nypl.org/locations/schwarzman +1 917 275 6975

106 STAVROS NIARCHOS FOUNDATION LIBRARY

455 5th Avenue, New York, New York 10016, USA

TO VISIT BEFORE YOU DIE BECAUSE

Sporting a striking 'wizard hat' roof, this state-of-the-art library on 5th Avenue boasts Manhattan's only free, publicly accessible roof terrace.

Just across the street from the main branch of the New York Library (page 173), this public library is the state's largest circulating branch. Designed by architects Mecanoo and Beyer Blinder Belle to complement its iconic, research-only neighbour, it is housed in the shell of the Mid-Manhattan Library, originally built in 1914 as a department store. At its heart is a welcoming triple-height atrium, with a vibrant ceiling artwork by Hayal Pozanti. On one side are day-lit reading areas; on the other are five levels of book stacks, visible to passers-by through the library's 40th Street windows. A window in the lower level allows visitors to see the book-sorting machine in action; it deals with around 2 million items returned by patrons each year. The teen section is decorated with bold murals by Melinda Beck, while some of the 20m-long bespoke tables throughout are supported by the building's original steel frame. A visit isn't complete without a trip to the rooftop terrace, where you can admire both the Midtown views and the dramatic aluminium roof.

nypl.org/locations/snfl

+1 212 340 0863

107 LITTLE FREE LIBRARIES

Thousands of locations worldwide

TO VISIT BEFORE YOU DIE BECAUSE

These humble little boxes of books celebrate the twin joys of reading and sharing. Bring a book, take a book – and build your own if you can.

There's one next to the South Pole in Antarctica, one in a 110-year-old tree in Idaho and another shaped like a saguaro cactus in Arizona. Some are built of wood, others of Lego. But it all started in 2009 in Hudson, Wisconsin, when former schoolteacher Todd H. Bol used wood from his old garage door to make the first library-on-a-stick as a tribute to his mother. His neighbours loved it, so Bol set himself a goal of 2,150 Little Free Libraries, to beat the number of Carnegie libraries in the country – a goal he achieved in 2012, the same year he founded the Little Free Library charity. Today there are more than 200,000 registered Little Free Libraries in 128 countries (and there's even a handy app to find the one nearest to you). Over 400 million volumes have been shared through the book-exchange boxes, which offer 24/7 book access and fight book poverty and illiteracy. There are many more unregistered street libraries, and every single one makes a difference.

littlefreelibrary.org

108 LIBRARY OF THE CANADIAN PARLIAMENT

111 Wellington Street, Ottawa, Ontario K1A 0A4, Canada

TO VISIT BEFORE YOU DIE BECAUSE

A flamboyant example of Gothic Revival, this octagonal marvel features ornate interiors with multicoloured ironwork and sculpted white pine panels.

The 'jewel in the crown of Parliament Hill', the 'grand old lady', 'Canada's most beautiful room' or even the 'wedding cake'... There's no shortage of nicknames to describe the Library of the Canadian Parliament. Completed in 1878, its design was influenced by Alpheus Todd, the librarian of the Legislative Assembly at the time. Inspired by Edward Edwards' *Memoirs of Libraries*, and the British Museum Reading Room (see page 46), he asked for a circular shape, a domed ceiling with skylights and tiered galleries. Crucially, he also insisted on fireproof iron doors – the library was the only part of the parliament building to survive a fire in 1916. Restored in 2006 to their original Victorian splendour, the three-tiered book stacks are home to treasures including the 1748 *A Voyage to Hudson's-Bay*, by Henry Ellis, and Audubon's amazing *Birds of America* illustrations. The library is currently closed, as the parliament building is undergoing a $4 billion upgrade due to be completed in 2031. In the meantime, you can 'visit' the building as part of a free virtual experience.

lop.parl.ca

109 PARKWAY CENTRAL LIBRARY

1901 Vine Street, Philadelphia, Pennsylvania 19103, USA

TO VISIT BEFORE YOU DIE BECAUSE

Chock-full of literary treasures and precious maps, this immense Beaux Arts landmark is a paradise for music lovers that welcomes 1 million visitors a year.

This vast temple to knowledge is split into a series of departments, some of them housed in classically decorated double-height halls. The rare book section offers rotating displays of works such as illuminated medieval manuscripts, letters by Charles Dickens and Edgar Allan Poe, classic children's books and even Mughal court paintings. More unexpectedly, the library is also home to a commercial-grade kitchen 'used to advance literacy through food and cooking', and the world's largest lending library of orchestral music, consisting of over 21,000 titles. Here, you can borrow scores for Broadway musicals or even an entire symphony, which comes in a specially designed box, but also actual instruments such as Suzuki Omnichords. There are also popular children's, teens' and fiction libraries, as well as a lecture hall. Originally designed by Julian Abele, a prominent African American architect, the 1927 building was renovated by Moshe Safdie, who turned the high-density book storage into flexible working spaces. Volunteers offer daily architectural tours of the building.

 freelibrary.org +1 833 825 5357

110 BURTON BARR CENTRAL LIBRARY

1221 N Central Avenue, Phoenix, Arizona 85004, USA

TO VISIT BEFORE YOU DIE BECAUSE

Built to stand the test of time and to respond to the surrounding desert landscapes, this library has become a destination to celebrate the summer solstice.

Inspired by Arizona's Monument Valley, the Burton Barr Central Library is home to a very special event every year at solar noon on the summer solstice. On that day, rays of sunlight coming through the skylights set alight the reading room's tall 'candlestick columns' with the illusion of blue flames. Designed by Will Bruder and opened in 1995, the library claimed the 2021 Twenty-five Year Award by the American Institute of Architects, who described it as 'an icon of late-20th-century modern architecture, a source of great civic pride for the region and an early adopter of critical sustainable strategies in public architecture'. Named after a tireless advocate and fundraiser for the library, the modular building features curved copper façades and is protected from the sun by computer-controlled louvres and fabric sails. Easily adapted to the changing demands of modern libraries, it is home to a five-storey Crystal Canyon atrium, a reflecting pool, a makerspace and the Rare Book Room, which includes a working 1800s Washington Printing Press.

phoenixpubliclibrary.org +1 602 262 4636

111 PALAFOXIANA LIBRARY

5 Oriente Núm. 5, Casa de Cultura del Estado de Puebla, colonia Centro 72000, Mexico

TO VISIT BEFORE YOU DIE BECAUSE

The oldest public library in the Americas, this perfectly preserved baroque library feels very much like a time capsule.

The conquistadors' arrival in Central and South America led not only to the decimation of their native populations but also to the near-total destruction of Aztec and Maya codices and Incan quipu-knotted records. These were replaced by the manuscripts and early books of 'new' libraries such as Biblioteca Palafoxiana in Puebla City's historic centre. Established in 1646 by the local bishop, Juan de Palafox y Mendoza, this UNESCO Memory of the World collection is home to 45,000 books and manuscripts, dating from the 15th to the 20th century. Impressively, the collection has survived all of Mexico's wars intact, and right from the start, its focus has been the sharing of knowledge: anyone who could read was allowed inside the seminary library. Restored after the 1999 earthquakes and accessed through huge carved doors, it is an atmospheric space filled with the fragrance of leather-bound books, arranged on three-tiered bookcases that wrap around the entire room. On the weekends, there are sometimes musical performances in the library's courtyard.

palafoxiana.com +1 222 232 3483

112 THOMAS CRANE LIBRARY

40 Washington Street, Quincy, Massachusetts 02169, USA

TO VISIT BEFORE YOU DIE BECAUSE

Dating from the golden age of library building, this cosy space combines Richardsonian Romanesque with later additions to form a bustling community hub.

If Boston's magnificent central library is 'the people's palace', then Quincy's Thomas Crane Library is 'the people's living room'. Both were built in the same area, in the same decade, but they couldn't be more different. In Quincy, readers can sit on cosy armchairs by a fireplace hand-carved with native plants, in a wood-panelled room with alcoves and stunning stained-glass windows by John La Farge. A small masterpiece, it is considered the finest library designed by Henry Hobson Richardson, one of the USA's first great architects with Louis Sullivan and Frank Lloyd Wright. Featuring Richardson's signature Romanesque entrance arch, it was built in honour of stone magnate Thomas Crane with a granite and brownstone façade. Completed in 1882, it has been sympathetically extended many times since. While the historic wing hosts wedding ceremonies and the Olmsted Lawn yoga classes, the later extensions offer a makerspace; movie matinees; story times in English, Arabic and Cantonese; and the Library of Things, including baking pans, record players and even a kayak.

113 ROYAL PORTUGUESE CABINET OF READING

Rua Luís de Camões 30, Centro, Rio de Janeiro, Rio de Janeiro 20051-020, Brazil

TO VISIT BEFORE YOU DIE BECAUSE

With its colourful books, turquoise walls, carved shelves and gilded finials, this showstopping library is as exuberant as the city's famed Carnival costumes.

When 43 Portuguese immigrants founded the Real Gabinete in 1837 to promote Portuguese culture in the newly independent country of Brazil, little did they know that 50 years later, they would move their prized collection into one of the most beautiful libraries in the world – a building so striking that over 180 years later it would go viral on social media... Designed by Portuguese architect Rafael da Silva e Castro in Neo-Manueline style, the Lisbon stone façade is inspired by the Portuguese capital's Jerónimos Monastery and adorned with statues of writer Luís de Camões and explorer Vasco da Gama. Open to the public since 1900, the iron-stack library and reading room features a stained-glass dome, dark bobbin furniture and ornate jacaranda bookshelves holding the largest collection of Portuguese literature outside Portugal. Among the thousands of volumes are the library's prized gems: a first edition of *Os Lusíadas*, Luís de Camões' 1572 epic; and the original manuscript of *Amor de Perdição*, written by Camilo Castelo Branco in 1861. Also amazing is the nearby 1810 National Library of Brazil.

www.realgabinete.com.br +55 21 2221 3138

114 GEISEL LIBRARY

University of California San Diego, 9500 Gilman Drive, La Jolla, California 92093, USA

TO VISIT BEFORE YOU DIE BECAUSE

Intended to look like hands holding up a stack of books, this striking 1960s brutalist library is full of surprises, including Dr. Seuss' archives and a working carillon.

Located at the heart of the University of California's San Diego campus, and reached by following a snake-shaped slate-tile path through an orchard, is what looks like the docking site for a spaceship. Designed in the late 1960s by William Pereira, the architect of San Francisco's Transamerica Pyramid, this concrete structure manages to be both monolithic and ethereal, thanks to its acres of coated glass panels. It has been known as the Geisel Library since 1995, when Audrey and Theodor Seuss Geisel (aka Dr. Seuss) donated $20 million – and the children's author and cartoonist's entire archives – to the institution. You can see some of his original drawings and notebooks in the exhibition gallery, where shows highlight some of the library's 7 million volumes. In the open-air forum, you'll find a statue of Dr. Seuss and his Cat in the Hat, but make sure to look up to admire the concrete lattice system on the underside of the cantilevered floors. At the top of the library is a carillon that chimes on the hour every weekday from 7am to 7pm. Come at noon on Fridays for a live concert.

library.ucsd.edu +1 858 534 0134

115 SESC POMPÉIA

Rua Clélia 93 Pompéia, São Paulo, São Paulo, 05042-000, Brazil

TO VISIT BEFORE YOU DIE BECAUSE

Lina Bo Bardi's trailblazing transformation of a factory into a cultural space helped set the tone for the reuse of industrial buildings all around the world.

At SESC Pompéia, you can read next to a meandering indoor water feature or an open fireplace in a public covered plaza, and then enjoy a lunch at a communal table, a beer on the large open deck or a community play in the theatre. This is all part of the transformation of a series of 1920s factories into a cultural centre – a 'social experiment' and 'citadel of leisure' by the pioneering architect Lina Bo Bardi, who sought to amplify the spontaneous activities already taking place in the abandoned buildings. She exposed bricks, restored the saw-tooth roof and added concrete walkways and bright pops of red to highlight original details. The result, completed in 1986 for the non-profit organisation SESC, is now a beloved São Paulo institution. Located on a mezzanine with raised reading areas and beautiful bespoke chess tables and furniture designed by Bo Bardi, the library is home to thousands of volumes arranged on industrial metal shelves. And if you are in São Paulo, make sure to also visit the wonderful Biblioteca Parque Villa-Lobos.

sescsp.org.br/servicos-sesc-pompeia/#biblioteca

116 ARABIAN PUBLIC LIBRARY

10215 E McDowell Mountain Ranch Road, Scottsdale, Arizona 85251, USA

TO VISIT BEFORE YOU DIE BECAUSE

This desert-inspired building comes with futuristic weathered-steel façades, award-winning bookshop-like interiors and a focus on wellbeing.

The Arizona desert's slot canyons and Monument Valley were shaped over millennia by powerful natural forces, and it's this gradual sculpting of sandstone by water that Richärd Kennedy Architects sought to capture with this library in Scottsdale. Completed in 2007, the building is arranged around a central courtyard, accessed via a steel-and-glass 'slot canyon'. Echoing the desert's red stone walls, the terracotta weathered-steel façades are designed to patinate gracefully over time, and are complemented by custom artworks by Norie Sato. Key to the building's success is its peaceful atmosphere (unless the local school is out!), with chatter dimmed down thanks to perforated wood panels, and natural light flowing through carefully positioned openings. Featuring a tranquil courtyard, the social hub is home to a 120,000-volume collection as well as a coffee bar, a bookshop, dedicated spaces for children and teens, and community programmes. It also features a very American library innovation: a drive-through window service for patrons who are in a hurry.

scottsdalelibrary.org/locations#arabian +1 480 312 7323

117 SEATTLE PUBLIC LIBRARY

1000 4th Avenue, Seattle, Washington 98104-1109, USA

TO VISIT BEFORE YOU DIE BECAUSE

Filled with art, murals and bold splashes of colour, this acclaimed diamond-shaped library is renowned for its many innovative features.

Once upon a time, libraries were seen as dusty, old-fashioned and under threat from both the digital world and a shrinking public realm. Dutch architect Rem Koolhaas and Seattle-based LMN Architects proved otherwise, and boldly so, with their dynamic steel-and-glass Seattle Public Library. When it opened in May 2004, more than 25,000 people lined up to experience it for themselves. A powerful statement on the importance of civic spaces and the sharing of knowledge in all its forms, it was called 'the most exciting new building it has been my honor to review' by *The New York Times*' critic Herbert Muschamp. Designed as a series of stacked platforms to capture natural light and offer unique views, it features a 'Books Spiral' displaying the entire non-fiction collection in a continuous, wheelchair-accessible run; a living room with 15m-high ceilings; practice rooms for musicians; and the famous Red Floor, painted in 13 different shades of red. Among the many artworks on display are a tactile maple floor by Ann Hamilton, carved with quotes from the World Languages books located on the same level, and an underwater mural by Will Schlough complete with octopus and starfish readers.

spl.org

+1 206 386 4636

640
630
620
620

118 SUZZALLO LIBRARY

4000 15th Avenue NE, Seattle, Washington 98195, USA

TO VISIT
BEFORE YOU DIE
BECAUSE

Follow the university students' footsteps up the atmospheric stone grand staircase to admire this library's resplendent Reading Room.

The 'jewel in the crown' of the University of Washington campus, the Suzzallo Library was built in 1926 in the Collegiate Gothic style and dazzles with its soaring vaulted ceilings, intricate stained glass and detailed sandstone carvings. Its main entrance is guarded by stone figures depicting 'Mastery', 'Inspiration' and 'Thought', while a magnificent staircase, with travertine treads worn by decades of use, leads to a vaulted hall housing one of the world's biggest books, *Bhutan* by photographer Michael Hawley, printed with a gallon of ink on a roll of paper longer than a football field. Measuring 19m high, 15m wide and 76m long, the Reading Room is a cavernous space filled with colourful details: its oak bookcases are topped with hand-carved friezes representing native plants of Washington State; its leaded-glass windows incorporate medallions representing Renaissance watermarks; and a pair of hand-painted globes bear the names of famous explorers. Along with its 1960s addition and adjoining Allen Library, it is home to 2 million volumes spanning all the major disciplines, with temporary exhibits showcasing some of its literary treasures.

lib.uw.edu/suzzallo +1 206 543 0242

119 ST. LOUIS PUBLIC LIBRARY

1301 Olive Street, St. Louis, Missouri 63103, USA

TO VISIT BEFORE YOU DIE BECAUSE

The work of renowned architect Cass Gilbert, the central branch of St. Louis Public Library is a textbook example of turn-of-the-century splendour that has evolved into a thoroughly modern community hub.

Taking up a whole city block, this 1912 Carnegie library is filled with incredible details, showcasing the trademark grandeur of the Beaux Arts and neoclassical styles of its architect, Cass Gilbert. A skyscraper pioneer also behind the city's art museum, the US Supreme Court Building and the Detroit Main Library (see 152), Gilbert really went big here, decorating the imposing Maine granite façade with 30 shields bearing the printers' marks of the likes of Gutenberg, Plantin and Baskerville. The interiors bring the Italian Renaissance straight to downtown St. Louis, with exquisite replicas of features from the Pantheon, the Vatican and Michelangelo's Laurentian Library. In 2012 the library was propelled into the 21st century thanks to an extensive yet subtle renovation by George Nikolajevich and Cannon Design, rewarded with the American Institute of Architects' highest honour. Instead of huge metal book stacks, the North Wing now houses a light-filled atrium, puzzling table and makerspace, while new public spaces include art exhibition spaces and a café. Join a tour to find out more.

slpl.org +1 314 241 2288

120 TOLEDO LUCAS COUNTY PUBLIC LIBRARY

325 N Michigan Street, Toledo, Ohio 43604, USA

TO VISIT BEFORE YOU DIE BECAUSE

Fans of art deco will love to hang out in the central court of this carefully restored and extended library reflecting the region's glass manufacturing history.

There is a cookie-cutter template for the 1940s-era American public building: the Folger Shakespeare Library in Washington, DC. The striking art deco library is only opened to the public once a year, but you will find its copies all around the country, including here in Toledo. The library's streamlined façade hides a central court designed by Hahn and Hayes, with a frieze of locally produced Vitrolite glass murals representing the history of arts and science. From the light fixtures down to the terrazzo floor, all of its original features have been beautifully preserved. Extended with a modern addition in 2001, the library was recently transformed by HBM Architects, who have celebrated the central court's original geometric motifs on everything from desks to cabinets. Upstairs are more colourful glass murals in the children's library, and the cosy wood-panelled Blade Rare Book Room. HBM's King Road Branch Library, based on the motion of turning pages of a book, and the Mott Branch by Buehrer Group, with its striking canopy roof, are also worth a look.

+1 419 259 5200

121 TORONTO REFERENCE LIBRARY

789 Yonge Street, Toronto, Ontario M4W 2G8, Canada

TO VISIT BEFORE YOU DIE BECAUSE

Known as Toronto's 'great living room', this 1970s landmark designed by Raymond Moriyama features flowing curves and a surprising hidden room.

The largest public library in Canada, the Toronto Reference Library spreads over 36,417 sq m, its curvilinear balconies wrapping around a central five-storey atrium. Raymond Moriyama described his pioneering design as an 'empty cup' that encourages users to fill the space with their own thoughts. The Canadian architect also spent a great deal of time considering the 'feel' of sound; there are strategically placed acoustic baffles as the public areas 'should be quiet, but not dead'. Every detail is carefully considered and a later renovation added a glass entrance and café inspired by Moriyama's original design. The TD Gallery showcases rare items from the library's special collections, located in a custom-designed rotunda on the top floor with what appears to be Sherlock Holmes' study, home to the Arthur Conan Doyle Collection. Toronto is packed with amazing libraries including the Thomas Fisher Rare Book Library, York University's Scott Library, the Kelly Library and the monumental Robarts Library.

torontopubliclibrary.ca/torontoreferencelibrary

+1 416 395 5577

INFORMATION

122 VANCOUVER PUBLIC LIBRARY

350 W Georgia Street, Vancouver, British Columbia V6B 6B1, Canada

TO VISIT BEFORE YOU DIE BECAUSE

Reminiscent of a Roman amphitheatre, this sandstone-coloured library comes with all the contemporary necessities, including a digital media lab and rooftop garden.

Unfurling over an entire city block, architect Moshe Safdie's Central Library features a curved façade inspired by Rome's Colosseum. Although pretty radical for the time, Safdie's project was the public's favourite in the design competition to replace Vancouver's overcrowded central library and opened in 1995 after 26 months of construction. Surrounded by a busy tree-lined piazza, it contains 1.1 million items in 17 languages, including sheet music, graphic novels, zines, plays, board games and video games. It is also a Musical Instrument Lending Library, with 320 instruments from around the world – from ukuleles to doumbeks, banjos and violins – on offer. In 2018, the building's top two floors were transformed into community gathering spaces. As well as a rooftop garden by landscape architect Cornelia Oberlander with unique views of downtown, there is an 80-seat family theatre, bright meeting rooms and a glass-walled reading room. Over 50 works by local artists, from conceptualist pieces of the 1970s to today's Indigenous art of resistance, can be found throughout.

vpl.ca

+1 604 331 3603

123 COAL CREEK LIBRARY

696 E 1719 Road, Baldwin City, Kansas 66006, USA

TO VISIT BEFORE YOU DIE BECAUSE

Established in 1859 by two inspiring young women with a passion for education, this tiny library is a slice of history, lovingly maintained by local volunteers.

The oldest subscription library in Kansas, Coal Creek Library was founded on Thanksgiving Day in 1859, when two teenage girls, Martha Cutter and Anna Soule, held a meeting with 22 other young people to start a library association for the moral, social and intellectual improvement of its members. 'At a time when women's opinions were not respected, they wanted something better for their future than the area's tremendous violence,' explain Marta Jardon and Mel Verhaeghe of the Santa Fe Trail Historical Society, who note that the violence was related to the issue of slavery started by the passing of the Kansas-Nebraska Act in 1854. 'To think that through so much bloodshed, they could start something that could last all these years.' The group first ordered 10 books at the cost of $10 (about $375 today), and the collection grew and grew, until in 1900 the entire community joined forces to build a new library to house over 1,000 books in tall oak bookshelves. Today, despite the state's destructive tornadoes, it still stands proudly as the red building at the heart of Vinland. It is open to the public on Sundays from April through October.

santafetraildouglas.org/coal-creek-library

124 LIBRARY OF CONGRESS

101 Independence Avenue SE, Washington, DC 20540, USA

TO VISIT BEFORE YOU DIE BECAUSE

Perched on Capitol Hill, the largest library in the world is home to a majestic reading room and a series of exhibitions that bring its unparalleled collections to life.

Connected by tunnels to the Capitol, the Library of Congress' Thomas Jefferson Building has been dazzling the public since its opening in 1897. Its Great Hall is home to a Gutenberg Bible and murals depicting the evolution of the written word, from Egyptian hieroglyphics to the printing press. A pair of marble staircases then lead visitors to a mosaic depicting Minerva, the Roman goddess of wisdom, and a gallery from which you can take in the Main Reading Room, where researchers work under a large dome surrounded by figures representing different areas of knowledge, eras and regions of the world. The David M. Rubenstein Treasures Gallery is dedicated to sharing the most interesting items from the collections, while an ongoing exhibition showcases the library of avid reader Thomas Jefferson, who once followed a version of a system created by British philosopher Francis Bacon to arrange his many books. Free timed-entry tickets are required to enter the library; try Thursdays from 5pm for a visit accompanied by happy hour drinks and access to the Main Reading Room.

loc.gov/visit +1 202 707 5000

125 MARTIN LUTHER KING JR. MEMORIAL LIBRARY

901 G Street NW, Washington, DC 20001, USA

TO VISIT BEFORE YOU DIE BECAUSE

This thoughtfully renovated landmark honours the legacies of both its original architect Ludwig Mies van der Rohe and civil rights leader Martin Luther King Jr.

Opened in 1972, Ludwig Mies van der Rohe's only public library was constructed in honour of the American civil rights leader it is named after. Standing on the shoulders of these two giants is Dutch architecture firm Mecanoo, tasked to transform it into a contemporary hub. The project 'reconciles the Mies building, the values of Martin Luther King, and what the library of the future must be', writes Francine Houben, Mecanoo's founding partner. 'We have made the MLKL more organic, more transparent and more open.' Reopened in 2020, the library celebrates the powerful simplicity of the original building. It now also has a new café, a public roof garden, an auditorium and a suite of community studios and workshops, as well as two new wood-lined staircases and much-improved acoustics. A continuous reading counter stretches along the windows forming part of a 220m-long 'Reading Ribbon' over multiple floors. There's a slide in the colourful children's library, while the Grand Reading Room is now a double-height space adorned with an installation by Xenobia Bailey.

dclibrary.org/plan-visit +1 202 727 0321

126 WINTHROP PUBLIC LIBRARY

112 Norfolk Road, Winthrop, Washington 98862, USA

TO VISIT BEFORE YOU DIE BECAUSE

Inspired by local hay barns and majestic trees, this beautiful library in rural north Washington State was built by the community, for the community.

Many libraries in the USA are supported by their own local charities. Here in the Methow Valley, the Friends of the Winthrop Public Library have spent five years helping to create a new building for their community. Its volunteers gathered hundreds of requests to identify patrons' needs, which Johnston Architects took on board to design 'Winthrop's ideal civic space'. Through multiple workshops and interviews, the team learnt that the priority was a building that was sustainable, durable and flexible, and created a 678 sq m library inspired by the area's farm buildings and powered by solar panels. Its wooden structure is left exposed, giving 'a delicate, yet strong impression'. Sliding doors laser cut with the names of 2,000 donors reveal an open-plan layout with mobile shelving and works by local artists, while a burnt cedar snag is the focal point of the reading room. A garden planted with fire-resistant species completes the site, which is also a clean-air community refuge during the region's frequent wildfire season.

ncwlibraries.org/locations/winthrop-public-library

+1 509 996 2685

PRESENTED TO THE CITY OF ADELAIDE

127 STATE LIBRARY OF SOUTH AUSTRALIA

Corner of North Terrace and Kintore Avenue, Adelaide SA 5000, Australia

TO VISIT BEFORE YOU DIE BECAUSE

A perfect example of a late Victorian-era library, it has rows of beautiful decorative wrought-iron balustrades and golden lanterns.

Located in the heart of Adelaide, the State Library spans three buildings, including the jaw-dropping Mortlock Wing, named after a generous benefactor. Opened in 1884 with 23,000 books and three members of staff, it was designed by colonial architect E.J. Wood and features a central atrium ringed by two galleries of wooden shelves and illuminated by a glass-domed lantern roof. Its board of governors was so pleased with the new grand chamber that they purchased a very expensive clock at Dent & Sons in London to complete it. It was a worthwhile investment: the timepiece still keeps excellent time today, although it needs to be wound up every week. The building now houses exhibitions, study areas and the library of Federalist Sir Josiah Symon, and the Royal Geographical Society. A place to 'reflect upon our identities, preserve our memories, and gather our knowledge', the State Library tells the stories of South Australia through published material, photographs, Indigenous collections and personal archives.

slsa.sa.gov.au

+61 8 7424 6300

128 TŪRANGA

60 Cathedral Square, Christchurch Central City, Christchurch 8011, New Zealand

---

TO VISIT BEFORE YOU DIE BECAUSE

Not only is this earthquake-proof library built to last, but its Māori-inspired design also celebrates the local community and reflects its users' suggestions.

Devastated by an earthquake in 2011, Christchurch has undergone an enormous transformation in the past decade. Tūranga, its new central library completed in 2018, is widely considered to be its most successful rebuild. Named after the Māori word for 'foundation' and designed by architects Schmidt Hammer Lassen and Architectus, Tūranga rests on a stone-clad podium decorated with Māori artworks. Featuring a seismic force-resisting system with flexible concrete walls that can rock without breaking, the building is cloaked in a perforated, golden aluminium veil. Viewpoints open onto culturally significant geographic landmarks, including the mountain ranges of Maungatere, while residents' suggestions, including a 'Harry Potter staircase', a coffee cart for parents and Lego for creative play and learning in the children's section, a recording studio and 3D printers, were all reflected in the finished building. From its welcoming entrance, decorated with graphics of local birds, to its roof terrace, this library is Christchurch's new beating heart.

my.christchurchcitylibraries.com/turanga

129 CRAIGIEBURN LIBRARY

75–95 Central Park Avenue, Craigieburn VIC 3064, Australia

TO VISIT BEFORE YOU DIE BECAUSE

Sustainably built, beautifully designed but also warm and friendly, this award-winning library has become a focal point for the community.

Just a couple of years after its opening, the Craigieburn Library near Melbourne won the inaugural title of IFLA Public Library of the Year in 2014, with the judging panel impressed by how 'the City of Hume has used a library to create a sense of belonging for all, as both a learning centre and a gathering place for the city'. It can also claim to be one of the outposts of Hume Libraries, Australia's Favourite Library Service in 2014. The library's success lies not only in its friendly team but also in the stunning architecture by Australian practice fjcstudio, led by Francis-Jones Morehen Thorp. Built out of locally sourced rammed earth, selected for 'its thermal properties and for its symbolic resonance, embedding the building in the very ground from which it rises', the lightweight steel and timber roof structures are conceived as a series of interlocking pavilions and also house an art gallery and café. Its double-height reading room is flooded with light yet protected by louvred roofs, which extend throughout into the landscape, creating verandas that can be used for markets and music events.

humelibraries.vic.gov.au

+61 3 9356 6980

130 YELLAMUNDIE LIBRARY

52 Scott Street, Liverpool NSW 2170, Australia

TO VISIT BEFORE YOU DIE BECAUSE

Inspired by the Georges River, this curvilinear library has been praised both for its stunning, sustainable design and its community engagement.

This library opened in 2023 as part of the Yellamundie Civic Place Library and Art Gallery, a $600 million revitalisation of Liverpool's civic centre. Its unique round shape and circular windows are inspired by the flowing waters of the Georges River, also known as Tuggerah, which has sustained the community for generations. Both calm and dynamic, 'the rippling surfaces of the new building invite movement and flow around it, creating diverse spaces for everyone', write its architects, fjcstudio, also behind the award-winning Craigieburn Library (see opposite page). Located at the end of a tree-lined street and featuring a sunken courtyard garden, Yellamundie (The Storyteller) is also a highly sustainable oasis of calm and shaded spaces, its welcoming curved form also intended to give 'a sense of gathering and embrace'. It spreads over 5,000 sq m and six levels, housing 2km of bookshelves holding 85,000 items. Its top-floor children's library comes with very popular wavy window seats, while the interior palette is all soft browns and greens, reflecting the local landscapes.

mylibrary.liverpool.nsw.gov.au +61 2 8711 7177

131 MARRICKVILLE LIBRARY

Patyegarang Place, 313 Marrickville Road,
Marrickville NSW 2204, Australia

TO VISIT BEFORE YOU DIE BECAUSE

Set in a former hospital, this immensely popular library is a sensitive heritage adaptation incorporating recycled bricks, natural ventilation and rainwater tanks.

Australian practice BVN has designed a spate of beautiful libraries, from Woollahra, a plant-filled community hub in Double Bay, to Darling Square, a hive-shaped space in a Kengo Kuma building. Our favourite so far is this project in the Inner West of Sydney. And we're not the only admirers – it has been widely awarded, including the 2021 Australian Library Design Award. It's a new landmark for the city, thanks to its oversized floating zigzag roof, inspired by the pitch of the site's existing building, the 1897 Marrickville Hospital. From timber windows to terrazzo flooring, many original features have been restored, while a glazed walkway connects the old wards with new floors and a historic art books gallery. With its huge timber columns and triple-height spaces, the main foyer certainly has the wow factor. But it's also a warm, welcoming space with a large wooden auditorium staircase on which to perch with one of the library's 85,000 books, and a sunken lawn and café for breaks and meetings.

innerwest.nsw.gov.au/explore/libraries +61 2 9392 5588

132 STATE LIBRARY VICTORIA

328 Swanston Street, Melbourne VIC 3000, Australia

TO VISIT BEFORE YOU DIE BECAUSE

The library's grand historic reading rooms have been expertly restored and carefully extended with state-of-the-art contemporary facilities.

Established in 1854 as the Melbourne Public Library, State Library Victoria is one of the first free public libraries in the world, created with the belief that access to knowledge was fundamental to a prosperous and civil society. This vision continues to be celebrated today in a series of stunning spaces, including the showstopping La Trobe Reading Room. The vast octagonal space boasts a soaring dome ceiling, which was the largest reinforced concrete dome in the world when it opened in 1913. Other highlights include the historic Ian Potter Queen's Hall (the original reading room, with tall white columns and patterned skylights) and new facilities, such as the Ideas Quarter, part of a much-lauded contemporary transformation by Architectus and Schmidt Hammer Lassen (also behind Tūranga in New Zealand; see page 212). Its collections comprise over 5 million items, ranging from 15th-century volumes retracing the trial and execution of King Charles I, to the infamous suit of armour worn by bushranger Ned Kelly during his final stand in 1880.

slv.vic.gov.au

+61 3 8664 7000

133 CITY OF PARRAMATTA LIBRARY (PHIVE)

5 Parramatta Square, Parramatta NSW 2150, Australia

TO VISIT BEFORE YOU DIE BECAUSE

Like a cascading amphitheatre in the centre of town, this library's colourful tessellated roof signals an open and welcoming public space.

Since 2023 a vibrant red sail has graced the western Sydney suburb of Parramatta, like a glowing red answer to the iconic, billowing white curves of the capital's opera house. The work of Manuelle Gautrand Architecture, this sustainably built library's vibrant roof is inspired by the local flora, while its shape aims to maximise sunlight, not only inside but also on the adjoining Parramatta Square. 'The carefully sculpted final volume gives the impression of literally bending under the passage of the sun across the sky,' explains the French architect. The 65,000-book-strong library is the thread uniting all the various programmes of the PHIVE building, which include a children's centre, a small theatre and meeting spaces, as well as a Keeping Place dedicated to local Indigenous artefacts and reserved for the Aboriginal Dharug people. The ground floor 'urban lounge' and café encourages an indoor-outdoor experience; stepped floors provide great views of the square; and the top-floor council chambers boldly cantilever over the adjoining historic town hall.

cityofparramatta.nsw.gov.au/phive/library +61 13 0005 5555

PHIVE

RETURNS

134 CITY OF PERTH LIBRARY

573 Hay Street, Perth WA 6000, Australia

TO VISIT
BEFORE YOU DIE
BECAUSE

Designed by the leading Singapore-based Australian architect William Kerry Hill, this 3,500 sq m library features a showstopping ceiling mural.

Kerry Hill Architects are better known for setting a new benchmark for tropical luxury hotels all around Asia. But here in Perth, the hometown of founder William Kerry Hill, the practice has designed a great public space as part of the redevelopment of the city's Cathedral Square. The first big civic project since the construction of Perth's concert hall in the 1970s, the cylindrical design is swathed in vertical fins. A main staircase wraps around the floors, including a triple-height reading room. The library boasts peaceful interiors clad in warm timber, as well as a fourth-floor terrace where children can sit on a bean bag under a central Tree of Knowledge. Undoubtedly, the centrepiece is a ceiling mural by artist Andrew Nicholls. Entitled *Delight and Hurt Not*, it depicts the final act of Shakespeare's *The Tempest*, illustrated with Western Australian flora and fauna. As well as popular kitten cuddling sessions and multicultural story times, one of the library's most cherished events is the singing of Noongar carols, which brings people together to celebrate the holiday season.

perth.wa.gov.au +61 8 9461 3500

135 STATE LIBRARY OF NEW SOUTH WALES

1 Shakespeare Place, Sydney NSW 2000, Australia

TO VISIT BEFORE YOU DIE BECAUSE

Known for its serene reading room and UNESCO-listed collections, it's the only library in Australia with a rooftop bar offering unique views of Sydney Harbour.

The oldest continuously operating library in Australia, with a history dating back to 1826, the State Library of New South Wales is located in the heart of Sydney, on the land of the Gadigal people of the Eora Nation. Behind its classical sandstone façade lies a series of surprising spaces, including a rooftop bar, a 'secret' wood-panelled library commemorating the great English playwright William Shakespeare, and the magnificent Mitchell Library Reading Room. Opened in 1942, it houses around 50,000 books on the region's history, with millions more stored seven floors beneath street level in temperature-controlled stacks. There are also exhibition rooms and a grand vestibule with a mosaic replica of the original Tasman Map (1642-1644) held in the library's extensive cartographic collection. The library holds the journals, letters and drawings created by those who travelled with the First Fleet of British ships to Australia, while its Amaze Gallery is filled with wonderful pieces. Past exhibits have included Albrecht Dürer's 1525 *Painter's Manual* and 1920s *Bib and Bub* comic strips.

sl.nsw.gov.au +61 2 9273 1414

136 NATIONAL LIBRARY OF NEW ZEALAND

70 Molesworth Street, Thorndon, Wellington 6011, New Zealand

TO VISIT BEFORE YOU DIE BECAUSE

Not just a concrete bunker, this library has a mission to preserve and protect the nation's memory, from Māori oral history to illuminated manuscripts.

Part of the New Zealand parliamentary precinct, the National Library of New Zealand is a striking 1980s brutalist design. Shaped like an inverted pyramid, it is said to have been inspired by Boston's controversial City Hall. Its bold, fortress-like exterior protects some extraordinary documents known as He Tohu – the Declaration of Independence of the United Tribes of New Zealand, Treaty of Waitangi and Women's Suffrage Petition. 'Our library also houses some excellent pieces by artists including Cliff Whiting, but I have a particular soft spot for the collection store areas, having spent significant time in the vast basement as a library assistant working for the Turnbull Library,' says Rachel Esson, the National Librarian Te Pouhuaki. A gift from merchant and book collector Alexander Turnbull, this wonderful collection includes some of the world's most important resources on the works of English poet John Milton. Refurbished in 2012, the library is now being linked by a bridge to a new archival building next door, opening in 2026.

137 ABU DHABI CHILDREN'S LIBRARY

Sheikh Rashid Bin Saeed Al Maktoum Street, Al Hosn, Abu Dhabi, UAE

TO VISIT BEFORE YOU DIE BECAUSE

Beautifully designed play spaces, cosy reading nooks and a host of hands-on learning programmes make this library a joy for children to explore.

With its Book Mountain auditorium seating dotted with palm trees; a wavy, dune-inspired play space with a jeep to climb on; the Creature Space, home to giraffes and imaginary creatures; and wooden tree houses surrounded by 'book streams' – this library in Abu Dhabi is a real paradise for young readers. The only library in the city solely dedicated to children, it was designed by Danish architects CEBRA, who liken it to 'a life-size pop-up book', where children can discover stories in a variety of formats and languages, try stop-motion animation or snuggle up with their favourite comic book. Aiming to foster creativity and spark a lifelong love for reading, its three storeys each has a theme inspired by the landscapes of the UAE. The library opened in 2019 as part of the refurbishment of Abu Dhabi's Cultural Foundation, a listed cultural centre of Bauhaus origins completed in 1981, next to the historic Qasr Al Hosn ('White Fort'). The building also features a rooftop terrace, a 900-seat theatre and cutting-edge visual arts exhibitions.

culturalfoundation.ae/en/childrenslibrary

138 LIBRARY OF AFRICA AND THE AFRICAN DIASPORA

1 Nii Afotey Agyin IV Avenue Frafraha-Accra,
Adenta Municipality, Accra, Ghana

TO VISIT
BEFORE YOU DIE
BECAUSE

This award-winning decolonised library, archive, writing residence and research institute is an empowering celebration of Africa's literary works and heroes.

Sometimes it's more about the librarian than the library, and Sylvia Arthur's Library of Africa and The African Diaspora (LOATAD) is a case in point. Open by appointment only, this passion project started in 2017, when Arthur, a British-Ghanaian cultural activist, saw a need for high-quality, culturally relevant literature and decided to share her collection of 1,300 books with the Ghanaian public. Today the library is home to over 4,000 volumes by writers from 44 of Africa's 54 countries, as well as Black authors from the Americas, the Caribbean and Europe. Sharing and preserving titles means empowering both readers and writers with the knowledge and joy of books and connecting them with previous generations and a variety of Black experiences; Ghanaian works are of course well represented. A Ford Global Fellow and National Geographic Explorer, Arthur also continues to document the life stories of West African women through an expansive oral archive and is looking to rehome her collection into a purpose-built library in time for its 10th anniversary in 2027.

loatad.org

139 ABREHOT

Arat Kilo, Addis Ababa, Ethiopia

TO VISIT
BEFORE YOU DIE
BECAUSE

A symbol of hope for the country, this strikingly contemporary library celebrating knowledge and wisdom is an homage to Ethiopian heritage.

Ethiopia boasts a rich and ancient literary culture, and now has a state-of-the-art library to showcase it. Opened in 2022 on a former park opposite the Ethiopian Parliament Building, this 19,000 sq m library aims to be a beacon of learning and knowledge (Abrehot means 'enlightenment' in Amharic). And although Ethiopia is currently experiencing some troubled times, Abrehot still shines bright as the largest library in the country. The work of ZIAS Design, it comprises a garden where you can read surrounded by water features and olive and sessa trees; a dedicated online learning zone; and a main, four-storey building that can hold up to 1.4 million books. Colourful details are inspired by the decorations on traditional Ethiopian clothing, and include bold orange plaster and columns adorned with patterns and calligraphy of the word 'tibeb' (wisdom) in 18 languages, including in the country's unique alphabet. It's worth mentioning that the country also boasts a stunning historic library in the ancient capital of Gondar, the 'Camelot of Africa'.

abrehot.org.et

+251 111 704 576

140 BIBLIOTHECA ALEXANDRINA

Bab Sharqi, Alexandria Governorate 21526, Egypt

TO VISIT
BEFORE YOU DIE
BECAUSE

Lost in antiquity, the ancient Great Library of Alexandria is reborn in this striking cultural centre, a UNESCO-supported project designed by Snøhetta.

Dedicated to recapturing the spirit of openness and scholarship of the original Great Library of Alexandria, Bibliotheca Alexandrina aims to be a place of dialogue, learning and understanding. The papyrus scrolls and Greek columns of the legendary library have been replaced by shelf space for up to 8 million books and internet archives stored on hundreds of computers, in a building by leading Norwegian architects Snøhetta. Its vast circular form next to the city's curved harbour symbolises the cyclical nature of knowledge, while its glistening roof recalls the ancient Alexandrian lighthouse. The façade of Aswan granite slabs was hand-carved with 4,000 characters from most of the world's known writing systems, including Braille and musical notes. Surrounded by reflecting pools, the 11-storey library contains a huge, terraced reading room, as well as art galleries, a manuscript restoration laboratory, a planetarium and four museums. The fascinating Antiquities Museum displays artefacts found during the construction of the library and statues fished out of the city's Eastern Harbour. Join one of the regular guided tours to find out more.

bibalex.org

+20 3483 9999

141 CENTRAL LIBRARY CAPE TOWN

Old Drill Hall, Parade Street, Cape Town, South Africa

TO VISIT BEFORE YOU DIE BECAUSE

This buzzing, much-loved cultural hub is set in a landmark Victorian building with an ornate metal arched roof and brightly painted walls.

If only we could replace all weapons with books, wouldn't the world be a better place? Well, Cape Town has made a start by transforming an old military drill hall dating from the 1880s into a new Central Library, just a short walk away from the Cape Town City Hall. Extended by the well-known Victorian architect Anthony de Witt in 1889, and later used for boxing matches, dances and drama productions, the building features a large steel arched roof and elaborate cast-iron fanlights and stairways. The library opened in 2008 after the basement was excavated to make room for a new children's library, professional archives, storage and research areas. The spacious ground floor and galleries house the main library – the city's only public library with books in all of South Africa's 11 official languages. Containing over 200,000 items, the collection covers all aspects of arts and crafts and is especially strong in African and South African art, photography, fashion and graphic design.

www.capetown.gov.za

+27 21 444 0983

142 THE LIBRARIES OF CHINGUETTI

Chinguetti Old Town, Mauritania

TO VISIT
BEFORE YOU DIE
BECAUSE

This handful of ancient libraries in the Sahara Desert have miraculously preserved thousands of key medieval manuscripts and historic documents.

The Sahara seems like an unlikely place to find precious books, but it is in fact a fertile ground for ancient knowledge. Thanks to the dry desert air and the perseverance of generations of librarians, fragile manuscripts have been preserved in the same dry-stone buildings they were left in for centuries by Islamic pilgrims on their way to Mecca. Today in the former trading post of Chinguetti, you can visit privately owned libraries where ancient parchments are kept on earthen shelves, in small wooden chests or in simple paper files. The small city is being swallowed up by the shifting desert sands, so who knows how long the libraries can endure? Meanwhile, the famous Timbuktu Manuscripts, in neighbouring Mali, were threatened not only by the desert but also by jihadi fighters, who disliked the more tolerant vision of Islam they showcased. Local librarians used donkey carts to smuggle their priceless collection to a secret, safe location. Amazingly, 40,000 of these ancient texts on subjects such as astronomy, law and medicine, showcasing Africa's greatest written legacy, have been digitised and translated with the help of Google Arts & Culture and are now publicly available online. Google Arts & Culture features over 3,000 cultural institutions in 90 countries around the world, many of which are libraries.

artsandculture.google.com

143 AFROTHÈQUE

61 Rue B, Dakar, Senegal

TO VISIT BEFORE YOU DIE BECAUSE

More than just books on shelves, this is a small but mighty cultural hub that spreads its founders' passion for Africa's literary and cultural wealth.

There are no special buildings or ancient manuscripts here at Afrothèque, but there is something equally precious, yet intangible: a passion for books, and for sharing them with as many readers as possible. Created by journalist Pape Malick Barros, the library is a 'haven of culture and tranquillity', say its users, who also praise its welcoming team of librarians. 'I was lucky to read many African authors, such as Léopold Sédar Senghor or Aimé Césaire, at a young age. And when you grow up with those references, you fall in love with literature,' says Barros. 'The idea is to prepare future generations for the next challenges facing Africa. And to restore this continent's dignity, we need to arm ourselves intellectually, to arm ourselves with science.' Set up in 2021 after a crowdfunding campaign, Afrothèque offers 7,000 books by authors from Africa, the Caribbean and the African diaspora. Here, you can meet authors, discover new books or genres, share knowledge and learn through debates, workshops and film clubs – the perfect place to broaden your horizons.

@afrotheque

+221 77 869 55 55

144 QATAR NATIONAL LIBRARY

District of Freedom, Education City, Al Luqta Street, Doha, Qatar

TO VISIT BEFORE YOU DIE BECAUSE

This state-of-the-art, open-plan library was designed by leading architect Rem Koolhaas as a monument to the enduring value of the book.

Resembling two pieces of paper that have been pulled apart and folded diagonally to create a shell-like structure, Rem Koolhaas' Qatar National Library was designed to maintain a connection to the world outside, and to allow a precise amount of daylight to enter. 'The direct sunlight that permeates the building, the open spaces, and the warmth that the library exudes make it a lovely place to work or study,' says Laala Y. Al-Jaber, the library's head of Humanities. A key hub for library and information services development across the Middle East and North Africa, Qatar National Library's mission is to preserve the nation's heritage. Its collection currently hosts over 1 million books in more than 15 languages, organised on bookshelves that appear to rise from the floor. As well as high-tech automated systems and a conservation laboratory, the library features a stunning marble-clad Heritage Library, home to precious Arabic manuscripts and historical photographs.

qnl.qa

+974 4454 0100

145 AL-QARAWIYYIN LIBRARY

Seffarine Square, Fez, Morocco

TO VISIT BEFORE YOU DIE BECAUSE

One of the oldest continually operating libraries in the world, the landmark Al-Qarawiyyin is hidden behind a maze of alleyways in the heart of Fez's historic medina.

Said to have been founded as a mosque in the 9th century by the pious daughter of a rich merchant, Al-Qarawiyyin University became one of the leading spiritual and educational centres of the Islamic Golden Age. Its library was officially opened by Sultan Abu Inan in 1349 and extended many times over the centuries, the latest transformations dating from the 1940s and 2010s. Its collection of 4,000 manuscripts includes a 9th-century copy of the Quran written on gazelle parchment; the original copy of Ibn Khaldun's *Al-'Ibar*, a historical encyclopaedia gifted by the author himself in 1396; and what could well be the world's oldest medical degree, awarded to a certain Abdellah Ben Saleh Al Koutami in 1207. The landmark building's green-tiled roofs are visible from miles away. While the mosque is reserved for Muslims only, the library, as well as a nearby madrasa college, are regularly open to all visitors. Beautiful wooden latticework separates the bookshelves from the grand reading room, where rows of tables sit under an ornate wooden ceiling, surrounded by colourful mosaics.

uaq.ma

+212 661 197 222

146 MUYINGA LIBRARY

Muyinga, Burundi

TO VISIT BEFORE YOU DIE BECAUSE

Designed by Belgian practice BC architects & studies, Muyinga's first library tells an important story about how to think and build differently.

Part of an inclusive school for deaf children in northern Burundi, this stunning 140 sq m library was built in 2012 through a participatory process, which not only allowed a transfer of architectural knowledge but also instilled a sense of pride in the community. Instead of importing costly materials and experts, the architects at BC architects & studies built it out of earth, employing a local labour force and supporting the local economy. After months of fieldwork spent studying local construction, they applied their findings to this project, engaging the students in the building process, which used dry-stone walls, compressed earth blocks masonry and baked clay tiles. A porch offers shelter from harsh sun and heavy rain, while inside you will find eucalyptus beams and walls plastered with unbaked clay and sand from the local valley. The children's library features a large sisal hammock, woven from plants found on the construction site and accessed through a bookshelf/ladder. It's a wonderfully welcoming and much-needed space for children who are often excluded from local stories and knowledge, transmitted mainly through oral traditions.

odedim.org

147 MARIAM'S LIBRARY

Mwanyanya, Zanzibar, Tanzania

TO VISIT
BEFORE YOU DIE
BECAUSE

Built in only 34 days on a tight budget, Mariam's Library shows that low-cost libraries can be as impactful as big landmark projects.

This inspiring children's library in Zanzibar is part of the Parallel Gives charitable programme, dedicated to community service and supported by volunteer experiences, from Kuwait-based architects Parallel Studio. 'The focus is not on size or advanced design technology,' says founder Mai Al Busairi, 'but on the lesson of how to contribute to the global community, how architecture can positively affect human development, and how we can inspire our colleagues, at least in our region, to spread such kindness, generally.' Built out of clay bricks, the library serves both the student and local communities of Mwanyanya's Beit Ras School. The perforated façade helps with natural ventilation, keeping the space cool in the summer, but also creates lovely shadows on the wooden bookshelves, while the clear corrugated roof filters the light. Filled with donated books, the floor-to-ceiling shelving is punctuated by a circular window that doubles as a little reading nook, while a stepped concrete seating area forms a stage for performances.

148 LIBERIAN LEARNING CENTRE

A.B. Tolbert Road, Paynesville, Monrovia, Liberia

TO VISIT BEFORE YOU DIE BECAUSE

Liberia turns a new leaf with this Canadian-funded and -designed library featuring a children's atrium as well as co-working and start-up spaces.

Books were a scarce resource for Leo Nupolu Johnson, an award-winning entrepreneur who lived through a decade of civil war before fleeing Liberia, spending years living in refugee camps where libraries amounted to shipping containers full of random storybooks. But after resettling in Canada in 2006, he stumbled upon Hamilton Public Library and resolved to build a state-of-the art equivalent in his war-torn home country. A decade in the making, the Liberian Learning Centre in Paynesville is the country's first postwar library. A project by Johnson's Empowerment Squared charity, its sloped roof harvests solar energy and rainwater, addressing the challenges of unreliable power and access to clean water. Local labour and materials were integral to its construction, while Hamilton Public Library provided advice and help. Johnson's hope is that it is the first of many outposts of a new national library system. Liberia is soon to be home to the Ellen Johnson Sirleaf Presidential Center. Designed by Atelier Masōmī, it will be the first presidential library in the world dedicated to a woman.

liberianlearningcenter.com

149 HOUSE OF WISDOM

Al Juraina 1, Sharjah, UAE

TO VISIT BEFORE YOU DIE BECAUSE

A library but also a popular tourist destination, the House of Wisdom is an urban oasis with beautiful gardens and its own bookshops, restaurant and café.

Built by the local sheikh to commemorate Sharjah being awarded the title of UNESCO World Book Capital in 2019, this state-of-the-art cultural hub features a greenhouse-like reading room inspired by the Al Ain Oasis, a private section with cosy pods for women, a children's play space, a high-speed book printer for self-publishers and of course a library, packed with over 90,000 books. Designed by Foster + Partners as a landmark for the city's new cultural quarter, it is signposted by a sculpture by British artist Gerry Judah, a contemporary take on the ancient Arabic scrolls that spirals up towards the sky. Completed in 2021, the two-storey building is equally remarkable, with a large floating roof cantilevering on all sides to create shade, and aluminium and bamboo screens filtering the low evening sun. The emphasis throughout is to connect the building to the surrounding gardens. Exhibitions showcase rare and valuable items, while events include edible engraving, 3D-printing and prototyping workshops, as well as multicultural story times for little ones.

houseofwisdom.ae

+971 6 594 0000

ΒΙΒΛΙΟΘΗΚΗ
'Εντύπων
ΣΙΝΑ.
6165
ΒΙΒΛΙΟΘΗΚΗ
'Εντύπων
ΣΙΝΑ.
6166
4254
ΒΙΒΛΙΟΘΗΚΗ
'Εντύπων
ΣΙΝΑ.
6167
4255
ΒΙΒΛΙΟΘΗΚΗ
'Εντύπων
ΣΙΝΑ.
6168
4256
ΒΙΒΛΙΟΘΗΚΗ
'Εντύπων
ΣΙΝΑ.
6169

150 SAINT CATHERINE'S MONASTERY

Saint Catherine, South Sinai Governorate 8730070, Egypt

TO VISIT BEFORE YOU DIE BECAUSE

One of the world's oldest continuously operating libraries, it is filled with early codices and precious icons and is part of an ancient Greek Orthodox monastery.

Built between 548 and 565 at the foot of Mount Sinai, where Moses is said to have encountered the burning bush, Saint Catherine's is far from a dusty museum. It is part of a living community, with the treasures of its library still today used by monks for prayers, services and study. Collected over 17 centuries, they include 3,300 manuscripts (some written on papyrus scrolls). The most famous is the 4th-century *Codex Sinaiticus*, the Christian Bible in Greek, of which the monastery retains 12 pages and some 24 fragments. There are also some 8,000 early printed books, such as first editions of Homer, Plato and the comedies of Aristophanes. While its monks are working on a critical edition of *The Ladder of Divine Ascent*, the library's ancient palimpsests are slowly revealing their secrets thanks to new multispectral imaging techniques. Renovated in 2017, the library is open by appointment only, but you can also visit the adjoining museum and marvel at Byzantine icons, ornate gospel books or the illuminated Book of Job.

sinaimonastery.com

+30 210 6454 923

© Photos

Library 01: Delfino Sisto Legnani e Marco Cappelletti / library 02: p. 14 Dokk1; p. 15 Martin Schubert / library 03: Drazen Lovric, iStock / library 04: LUCID / library 05: Jesú Granada and Pol Viladoms / library 06: Stefan Müller / library 07: Nikada, iStock / library 08: p. 22 Stabi Berlin, 2022; p. 23 (top) Stefan Milivojevic, iStock; p. 23 (bottom) Jan Frontzek - Staatsbibliothek zu Berlin / library 09: Christian Richters / library 10: Daniel B. Harcz Fine Art Photography / library 11: James Kirwan, The Master and Fellows of Trinity College, Cambridge / library 12: courtesy of Joanina Library / library 13: urbazon, iStock / library 14: p. 30 (top) Noor Radya Binti MD Radzi, Shutterstock; p. 30 (bottom) Sean Fleming, iStock; p. 31 Liz Leyden, iStock / library 15: p. 32 (top) Tuomas Uusheimo - City of Helsinki; p. 32 (bottom) Daniel Leiviska - City of Helsinki; pp. 33-35 Kuvio - City of Helsinki / library 16: Virpi Peltola - City of Helsinki / library 17: John Crawford - Eas Mor Ecology / library 18: Erik Levilly - Ville du Havre / library 19: p. 40 (top) Santiago Rodriguez Fonto, iStock; p. 40 (bottom) Kutredrig, iStock; p. 41 jan van der Wolf, iStock / library 20: poludziber, Shutterstock / library 21: p. 43 courtesy of the British Library; pp. 44-45 Sam Walton, courtesy of the British Library / library 22: claudiodivizia, iStock / library 23: OlyaSolodenko, iStock / library 24: soniabonet, iStock / library 25: reproduced with permission of Chetham's Library, Manchester / library 26: The John Rylands Library, The University of Manchester / library 27: Marco Rothbrust / library 28: RomanBabakin, iStock / library 29: Erik Thallaug / library 30: Chunyip Wong, iStock / library 31: olrat, iStock / library 32: p. 56 Jerome Labouyrie, iStock; p. 57 Christine944, iStock / library 33: courtesy of the Bibliothèque Sainte-Geneviève / library 34: Eugeni Pons - Dominique Coulon & associés / library 35: National Library of the Czech Republic / library 36: Leonid Andronov, iStock / library 37: TadejZupancic, iStock / library 38: Daria Scagliola - Bibliotheek de Boekenberg / library 39: Stiftsbibliothek St.Gallen / library 40: p. 70 Thorir Ingvarsson, iStock; p. 71 Christina Vartanova, iStock / library 41: Stadtbibliothek Stuttgart, photo martinlorenz.net / library 42: The Hague & Partners Arjan de Jager / library 43: Ossip Architectuurfotografie / library 44: Staatliche Schlösser und Gärten Baden-Würtemberg, Günther Bayerl / library 45: Kees Hummel / library 46: Robtoz, iStock / library 47: IvanRossi - Fondazione Biblioteca Capitolare di Verona / library 48: p. 84 Austrian National Library - Hloch; p. 85 Austrian National Library - Pichler / library 49: Jeroen Pulles - DePetrus / library 50: Yuestock, Shutterstock / library 51: Akita International University / library 52: Alif Laila Book Bus Society / library 53: W Workspace / library 54: Zhu Yumeng Snøhetta / library 55: jixiediyigan, iStock / library 56: Arch-Exist Photography / library 57: Nguyen Thai Thach & An Viet Dung, all copyrights belong to Farming Architects / library 58: Photogilio, iStock / library 59: Mustafa Hazneci - Salt Research / library 60: saiko3p, iStock / library 61: KIE Arch / library 62: Kanazawa Umimirai Library / library 63: p. 108 Pavliha, iStock; p. 109 (top) Pavliha, iStock; p. 109 (bottom) straannick, iStock / library 64: Takuya Seki / library 65: CC By-SA 2.0, JSW Group, www.flickr.com/photos/198586615@N08/52976396686 / library 66: ZZ3701, iStock / library 67: Osaka Convention & Tourism Bureau / library 68: Su Shengliang, Chen Hao, Xia Zhi / library 69: CC BY-SA 3.0, Front view of Rampur Raza Library, Deepak G Goswami, https://commons.wikimedia.org/wiki/Category:Raza_Library#/media/File:Front_view_of_Rampur_Raza_Library.jpg / library 70: p. 117 Elena Sergejeva, iStock; pp. 118-119 dem10, iStock / library 71: Jongno Foundation for Arts & Culture / library 72: Jae Young Ju, iStock / library 73: RAWVISION studio / library 74: Jin Weiqi / library 75: Ethan Lee / library 76: Kuo-Min Lee / library 77: coward_lion, iStock / library 78: Ishiguro Photographic Institute / library 79: Zhang Chao / library 80: Kawasumi-Kobayashi Kenji Photograph Office / library 81: University of Michigan Law School / library 82: Leonid Furmansky - Austin Public Library / library 83: John Lehr / library 84: JerryPDX, iStock / library 85: Nic Lehoux / library 86: p. 144 (top) Neil Zeller; p. 144 (bottom) Calgary Public Library; p. 145 Michael Grimm / library 87: vertuio, iStock / library 88: Cleveland Public Library / library 89: Lara Swimmer / library 90: benedek, iStock / library 91: EJ_Rodriquez, iStock / library 92: Kathryn Dowgiewicz / library 93: Chevalier Morales Architects / library 94: Phillips Exeter Academy / library 95: JAG Studio / library 96: Ramiro del Carpio / library 97: Juan Jose Napuri, iStock / library 98: S Gomez - El Equipo Mazzanti / library 99: mofles, iStock / library 100: iStock / library 101: Lara Swimmer / library 102: BAnQ - Mikaël Theimer / library 103: p. 170 Michael Marsland for Beinecke Library, Yale University; p. 171 (top) Beinecke Library, Yale University; p. 171 (bottom) Tubyez Cropper for Beinecke Library, Yale University / library 104: Kurka Geza Corey, Shutterstock / library 105: courtesy of The New York Public Library / library 106: copyright by John Bartelstone, courtesy of Mecanoo and Beyer Blinder Belle / library 107: Little Free Library® is a registered trademark of Little Free Library, a 501(c)(3) nonprofit organization, and is used with its permission / library 108: Steven_Kriemadis, iStock / library 109: J. Smith for VISIT PHILADELPHIA® / library 110: Phoenix Public Library / library 111: al_la, iStock / library 112: Henry Cheung / library 113: p. 184 dabldy, iStock ; p. 185 luoman, iStock / library 114: Thomas De Wever, iStock / library 115: Antonio Salaverry, Shutterstock / library 116: Bill Timmerman / library 117: Lara Swimmer / library 118: photos courtesy University of Washington / library 119: Timothy Hursley - St. Louis Public Library / library 120: Roger Mastroianni / library 121: Toronto Public Library / library 122: Vancouver Public Library / library 123: Marta Jardon / library 124: Library of Congress / library 125: p. 206 Robert Benson; p. 207 (top) Robert Benson; p. 207 (bottom) Trent Bell / library 126: p. 208 Lara Swimmer; p. 209 Benj Drummond / library 127: Steven Liu, 2006 and Toby Woolley, February 2010, SLSA: B 74136 / library 128: Christchurch City Council / library 129: Trevor Mein / library 130: Brett Boardman / library 131: Tom Roe, courtesy of BVN / library 132: Yeoseop Yoon / library 133: p. 221 Sara Vita; pp. 222-223 Brett Boardman / library 134: The City of Perth / library 135: Mitchell Library Reading Room - image by Daniel Boud, courtesy State Library of NSW / library 136: Mark Beatty / library 137: courtesy of Department of Culture and Tourism - Abu Dhabi / library 138: Seth Avusuglo - LOATAD / library 139: Jami Hassen / 140: p. 232 Emily_M_Wilson, iStock; p. 233 (top) Gargolas, iStock; p. 233 (bottom) murat4art, iStock / Library 141: Cape Town Central Library / library 142: HomoCosmicos, iStock / library 143: Afrothèque / library 144: Shadi Ghonim / library 145: ugurhan, iStock / library 146: BC Materials & studies / library 147: Nassor Othman - Parallel Studio / library 148: Empowerment Squared / library 149: Chris Goldstraw / library 150: p. 250 (top) Romeo Ninov, iStock; p. 250 (bottom) Diy13, iStock; p. 252 Diy13, iStock / Back cover: Jason Varney

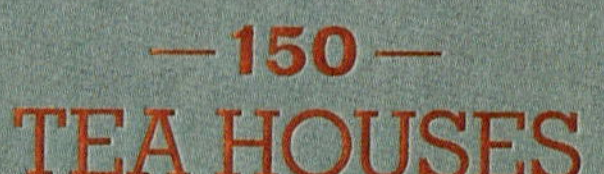
— 150 —
TEA HOUSES
YOU NEED
TO VISIT BEFORE
— YOU DIE —
A selection of the 150 most
exquisite tea houses
in the world — each having
a unique *story to tell*.
From the United Kingdom
to Japan and from
Morocco to Chile.
By Léa Teuscher — *Enjoy!*
Lannoo
150 | HOUSES | YOU NEED TO VISIT BEFORE YOU DIE
150 | WINE BARS | YOU NEED TO VISIT BEFORE YOU DIE
150 | HOTELS | YOU NEED TO VISIT BEFORE YOU DIE
150 | GOLF COURSES | YOU NEED TO VISIT BEFORE YOU DIE
150 | BOOKSTORES | YOU NEED TO VISIT BEFORE YOU DIE
150 | RESTAURANTS | YOU NEED TO VISIT BEFORE YOU DIE
150 | SPAS | YOU NEED TO VISIT BEFORE YOU DIE
150 | VINEYARDS | YOU NEED TO VISIT BEFORE YOU DIE
150 | NATIONAL PARKS | YOU NEED TO VISIT BEFORE YOU DIE
150 | BARS | YOU NEED TO VISIT BEFORE YOU DIE
150 | GARDENS | YOU NEED TO VISIT BEFORE YOU DIE

IN THE SAME — SERIES —

150 Tea Houses You Need to Visit Before You Die
ISBN 978 90 209 2661 3

—

150 National Parks You Need to Visit Before You Die
ISBN 978 94 014 1970 3

—

150 Spas You Need to Visit Before You Die
ISBN 978 94 014 9747 3

—

150 Vineyards You Need to Visit Before You Die
ISBN 978 94 014 8546 3

—

150 Bookstores You Need to Visit Before You Die
ISBN 978 94 014 8935 5

—

150 Gardens You Need to Visit Before You Die
ISBN 978 94 014 7929 5

—

150 Bars You Need to Visit Before You Die
ISBN 978 94 014 4912 0

—

150 Wine Bars You Need to Visit Before You Die
ISBN 978 94 014 8622 4

—

150 Houses You Need to Visit Before You Die
ISBN 978 94 014 6204 4

—

150 Golf Courses You Need to Visit Before You Die
ISBN 978 94 014 8195 3

—

150 Hotels You Need to Visit Before You Die
ISBN 978 94 014 5806 1

—

150 Restaurants You Need to Visit Before You Die
ISBN 978 94 014 9570 7

Texts
Léa Teuscher

Editing
Heather Sills

Book Design
ASB (Atelier Sven Beirnaert)

Typesetting
Keppie & Keppie

Back cover image
Jason Varney

www.lannoo.com
THEMA: WTH, AMG
D/2025/45/431
ISBN 978-90-209-3103-7

Sign up for our newsletter with news about new and forthcoming publications on art, interior design, food & travel, photography and fashion as well as exclusive offers and events. If you have any questions or comments about the material in this book, please do not hesitate to contact our editorial team: art@lannoo.com